The First Resurrection: The Historic Hope of the Church

By
Chad Stewart
and
Steven Eleftheriadis

Copyright © 2018 Chad Stewart and Steven Eleftheriadis

All rights reserved.

No portion of this book may be reproduced, stored in a retrieval system, or transmitted by any means except for brief quotations in critical reviews or articles, without the prior written permission of the author.

ISBN: 978-0-9958288-4-1

Published by Millennial Word Publications 2018
www.mwordpublications.com

Acknowledgement

The Bible says that, " … no one can lay a foundation other than that which is laid, which is Jesus Christ" (1 Corinthians 3:11).

This book, which we are privileged and honored to write, attempts to lay no new doctrine, plant no bad seed, nor detract from the manifest presence, glory and power or our Lord and Savior Jesus Christ.

Jesus is at the center of our faith and our hope for eternal life. Whatever your views regarding the end-times are, it is important for us to acknowledge that without Christ's birth, suffering, death, and resurrection, we are all dead in our sins, first last, and always.

Arguments about the meaning, purpose, and timing of the 'Rapture' or the Resurrection, therefore, mean nothing without salvation. If you are not saved; if you are not a believer in Jesus Christ and have not received Him by faith as Lord and Savior, this book will have little meaning or use for you.

For those who have, however, we wish to acknowledge on these pages that the work we have endeavoured to produce is not our work alone but of many who came before us. In this regard we are not creating anything new, any more than someone mining for gold actually 'creates' the gold. Rather we are simply attempting to bring to light the truths found in Scripture and which have either lain there, undisturbed, all along, or have been misinterpreted.

In this regard we have been blessed to merely build upon the foundation of sound doctrine going back to the writers of the Bible and the early church fathers. It is from their efforts, and the wisdom that has been imparted through events like The Reformation, which produced works of theology such as the Institutes of the Christian Religion (Calvin), Theological Common Places (Melanchthon) the works of Martin Luther, etc., that we even have an opportunity to do anything at all.

Yet their works, though not necessarily specific to the subject we are about to tackle, are themselves of no value if they do not encourage, inspire, and promote a greater understanding of " … the faith that was once for all delivered to the saints (Jude 3). That faith, however, is less than meaningless if not grounded on the reality, presence, and power of our Lord and Savior Jesus Christ.

Our first acknowledgement, therefore, must be to our Lord Jesus Christ, who we pray is found to be at the center of this work, as He is the center of God's plan of salvation for mankind. Likewise we wish to acknowledge the many kind people in our lives that God has blessed us with, and from whom, over many years, have sustained us in this effort.

Chief among these people must be our spouses, who have shown great patience with us as we struggled to put this together over many months and even years.

Summer Stewart is not only a wife and mother to four wonderful kids, but a sister in the Lord. Her grace, wisdom, and understanding as her husband engaged in this work are rivalled only by her manifest faith in Jesus. To her a debt is owed that goes beyond merely being a supportive wife, but also being a source of great strength and undying affection, one that her husband has no words to adequately express.

Marion Eleftheriadis deserves not only great credit for her careful edits of every page of this book but, some would say, of being brave enough to marry one of the authors. Through many days and weeks, she read this book as it was coming together, highlighting omissions in spelling, grammar, and context, as well as offering sound advice and honest criticism. What is most astonishing about her is that she does these things without thought of reward or hint of pride. Indeed, it took some convincing to even allow her to accept even this acknowledgement (poor reward though it is) for her invaluable contribution and effort.

To both these women—these lovely ladies who have encouraged us in this work—and whom we are blessed to have in our lives, we fondly express our love, our most sincere admiration for all they have gladly put up with. As the Scriptures say, "Charm is deceitful, and beauty is vain, but a woman who fears the LORD is to be praised" (Proverbs 31:30).

Beyond these we also wish to that Pastor Larry E. Wilson, recently retired from the Orthodox Presbyterian Church; his last post held at Redeemer Orthodox Presbyterian Church in Airdrie, Alberta, Canada, who offered us a quote used in this book and who provided sound counsel on various sections of it. Even though he would consider himself in a different eschatological 'camp' from the authors he is a true brother in the Lord and has served Him faithfully for the majority of his life.

We also wish to thank our friends who, over the years, have helped shape our understanding of the Bible. Among them are James Parker, Dirk and Carla Hildebrandt, as well as Rudy and Jen Schinschick, and many others too numerous to list here.

There are many others, not listed, including old Pastors, who guided and nourished our faith over the years; numerous authors and writers whose works we, again, are building on, as well as our extended families too. You are all in our hearts and we love you.

Lastly, we wish to acknowledge you, our readers, who spent money and time to buy and read this book. You have taken a great leap of faith by entrusting us with your hard-earned money in buying this work and we pray you do not believe it was in vain. Were it up to us, we would gladly give it away. It is, however, as Scripture says that the laborer is worthy of his hire (Luke 10:17). Being conflicted by these two ideas we have, however, kept the cost low so that all who would like to, could afford a copy of this work.

May it bless you in your understanding of end-times.

In Christ,

Chad Stewart
And
Steven Eleftheriadis

Introduction

The Resurrection of Believers is a critical doctrine that has sustained the hope of Christians since the earliest days of the Church. According to the Apostle Paul the preaching of the resurrection of Believers is done, in part, to comfort weary Christians as they pilgrim through this present wicked world. This is why he instructed the Thessalonian church to " ... encourage one another with these words" about the Resurrection (1 Thessalonians 4:18).

That Scripture, however, was not written solely for the benefit of those early Christians, who found themselves surrounded by the pagan Roman world, but also for us. It transcends both the time(s) and the people it was written for, which is why Paul says *all Scripture* is profitable, " ... for teaching, for reproof, for correction, and for training in righteousness" (2 Timothy 3:16).

The encouragement in Thessalonians comes from the knowledge that, one day, those dear saints who have fallen *asleep* in Christ will be reunited with those who are alive at the time of Christ's second coming. Paul even told the Thessalonians, "But we do not want you to be uninformed, brothers, about those who are asleep, that you may not grieve as others do who have no hope." (1 Thessalonians 4:13).

It is exceedingly assuring for Christians to know that, one day, we will be stripped of our mortality and will put on immorality (1 Corinthians 15:52-53). We can see this teaching exemplified in the Apostle John's writings where he wrote, "Beloved, we are God's children now, and what we will be has not yet appeared; but we know that when he appears we shall be like him, because we shall see him as he is … " (1 John 3:2).

In the last 150 years or so, however, there has been much confusion in evangelical circles surrounding this event. The confusion we speak of is not in regard to whether or not the Resurrection will take place, but rather when.

Some theological liberals, and other apostates, actually deny that Christ will return at all, claiming that they cannot accept any teaching which is supernatural in scope. In this book we are not addressing those who are in this category. We are, rather, writing to those who hunger for the things of God, who have been saved from the wrath to come, and who desire to know the truth.

There are four main prophetic positions within the end-times debate that need to be mentioned at this point. These positions are: Ammillennialism, Postmillennialism, Dispensational Premillennialism, and Historic Premillennialism. All of them, historically, share a common belief in a resurrection of the wicked and the righteous, and that Christ is returning visibly, physically, and through the clouds. But there are some critical differences as well.

These differences are broadly understood as belonging to the field of biblical study known as 'eschatology' which the Oxford Dictionary defines as, "The part of theology concerned with death, judgement, and the final destiny of the soul and of humankind."[1]

Differences in eschatology are not quite the same thing as having a difference in soteriology (the 'doctrine of salvation'[2]), which most of these positions share in common. Our intent is to explain the four main eschatological positions, and how they diverge from each other, not the latter.

---

[1] https://en.oxforddictionaries.com/definition/eschatology

[2] https://en.oxforddictionaries.com/definition/soteriology

These divergences include questions such as, "Will there be a thousand year period called the 'Millennium,' where Christ will rule upon the earth? How do Israel and the Church fit into God's end-time plan? Will there be a period of tribulation in the future, and, if so, will the resurrection of Believers happen before this tribulation (known as the Pretribulation Rapture) or after (known as the Post tribulation Rapture)? And, finally, which view does Scripture clearly teach?"

As we discuss these main points of contention, we will be focusing most of our attention on the Dispensational and Historic Premillennial views, explaining them in the light of Scripture. In the process we will also go through many of the writings of well-known so-called 'prophetic' teachers (those currently active, as well as those from the near and distant past), along with the testimony of many of the early church fathers to ascertain, by God's grace, which position is the most biblical.

Phillip Schaff, a Protestant theologian and church historian said, in reference to the Protestant's method of discovering truth from God's Word, "Evangelical Protestantism makes the Scripture alone the supreme rule, but uses tradition and reason as means in ascertaining its true sense."[3] This methodology we hope to emulate in this work.

So now you might be asking yourself, "Why, in a world drowning in prophetic literature, would anyone want write yet another book in this already congested field of study?" To answer this, we must first say that we are troubled about the theological landscape of the Church and are genuinely concerned about the dominant stream of eschatology that is being taught today. Secondly, we see serious Biblical problems with the most popular position being disseminated throughout the Church today. Lastly we are profoundly worried about the deeper theological implications of this position, (which are quite serious) and their enduring impact upon sound doctrine, should they continue to be taught without a sound exegesis as to their outcome for Believers.

For this reason we believe that it is good and right for us, and all Christians, to look into the issues at hand. Our main focus, however, will revolve around the system of theology known as 'Dispensationalism' and how this has contributed to the eschatological differences we hope to address here.

---

[3] Schaff, History of the Christian Church, Vol. 7, pg. 26

Please understand that our prime motivation is not to start a controversy (although this is quite probable given the level of intensity which is put into the topic of prophecy today), but rather, to encourage Christians to think about what the Holy Scriptures teach. We want Christians to better understand what they read in the Bible, to reason through texts, and properly connect them in order to come to a greater understanding of God's truth. In other words, we want Christians to not only think in terms of Sola Scriptura (Scripture alone) but also by Toto Scriptura (total Scripture).

As it was in the early days of the Church we would like to encourage open discussion and dialogue on this topic, which can be highly contentious among Believers. By so doing we hope to 'hammer it out' (so-to-speak), and come to a fuller appreciation of what God's Word has to say about the Resurrection.

All too often we Christians appear very willing to believe what we are taught in church, and elsewhere, without first diffusing it through the prism of Scriptural truth (this has been our experience, too). We encourage you, therefore, as sincere believers in Christ, and in His Word, to carefully analyze the things you have been taught so far and see if they really are of God.

Once proved you can cherish those doctrines and live by them. If, however, they are not of God you will have given yourself an opportunity to abandon error and cleave to the truth, satisfied in the knowledge of having wielded the sword of the Spirit, which is the Word of God, as a fit soldier of Jesus Christ, " … being trained in the words of the faith and of the good doctrine that you have followed." (1 Timothy 4:6).

1

The Four Main Prophetic Positions

Before we begin our study of the system of theology known as Dispensationalism and the doctrine of the Resurrection, we felt that it would be prudent to take a brief but concise look at the four main prophetic positions in existence today.

Amillennialism:

The term Amillennialism simply means 'no millennium.' But as at least one pastor has told us, that meaning "does not do justice to the term."[4] The reason is that Amillennialists do, in fact, believe in a millennium; it's just a lot different than the Premillennialists understanding.

Calvinist minister and theologian, Anthony A. Hoekema, wrote, in connection with this idea of amillennialism, "The term amillennialism is not a happy one. It suggests that amillennialists either do not believe in any millennium or that they simply ignore the first six verses of Revelation 20, which speaks of a millennial reign. Neither of these two statements is true. Though it is true that amillennialists do not believe in a literal thousand-year earthly reign which will follow the return of Christ, the term amillennialism is not an accurate description of their view. Professor Jay E. Adams of Westminster Seminary in Philadelphia has suggested that the term amillennialism be replaced by the expression realized millennialism. The latter term, to be sure, describes the amillennial position more accurately than the usual term, since amillennialists believe that the millennium of Revelation 20 is not exclusively future but is now

---

[4] Larry Wilson, Retired Pastor, Orthodox Presbyterian Church

in process of realization. The expression realized millennialism, however, is a rather clumsy one, replacing a simple prefix with a three-syllable word."[5] Unfortunately, as Hoekema himself realized, we are stuck with the term Amillennialism and must, therefore, continue to make use of it when discussing the different prophetic positions. That said, it has been (and still is), the officially recognized identity for those who hold to the position, even though it is probably not the most accurate description of their view.

Interestingly enough, the amillennialist view was not recognized as a distinct position until around the turn of the 20th century. Until then they were actually considered postmillennial because of their view that Christ would return at the end of the millennium.

Kim Riddlebarger, in his book, 'A Case for Amillennialism: Understanding the End Times', says, "Dutch statesmen and theologian Abraham Kuyper (1837-1920) may have been the first to use the term 'amillennial'."[6] There are, however,

---

[5] Hoekema, The Meaning of the Millennium: Four Views, pg. 155, InterVarsity Press

[6] Riddlebarger, A Case for Amillennialism: Understanding the End Times, pg. 31, Baker Books

distinct differences between Postmillennialism and Amillennialism; differences which will become more apparent as we proceed with our study.

As we noted earlier, Hoekema says that the Amillennialists think that, "the millennium of Revelation 20 is not exclusively future but is now in process of realization." In other words, the millennium is actually occurring now; that is, it is being realized in the reign of Jesus Christ in Heaven and through the work of the Church on Earth. Furthermore, they believe that the promises made to Israel in the Old Testament are fulfilled by Jesus Christ and his Church by the preaching and spread of the Gospel.

To the Amillennial, the thousand years described in Revelation 20 are largely figurative, existing between the two advents of Christ. In the first advent, Christ came and bound Satan through His victory at the cross. To them, this event started the symbolic 'thousand year reign of Christ,' which is an indeterminate period, until He comes back. When He does, this will mark the end of the first advent and the beginning of the second.

It is in this period that Satan will be loosed and Christ will come back in judgement. Also at this time, the general resurrection will occur, Christ will judge all people, and then He will establish a new heaven and new earth.

Postmillennialism:

The Postmillennial view is the most optimistic position of all the prophetic views. As the term suggests, Postmillennialists believe that Christ will return at the close of the millennium described in Revelation. Like the Amillennialist most Postmillennialists view the thousand years as symbolic and not a definite period. Unlike the Amillennialist, however, they believe that the world is to be Christianized before the second coming of Christ.

According to their beliefs, the kingdom of God is being extended in the world through the preaching of the Gospel and the work of the Holy Spirit. The entire world will eventually be reformed through the salvation of the majority of mankind.

This will effectively bring an outward change to the world through a social, political, and cultural transformation. It also brings about the start of the millennium where there will be a thousand years (either actual or symbolic) of peace and righteousness. Postmillennialists are divided, however, as to when the millennium will start, or whether it will start abruptly or gradually.

Reformed theologian, Loraine Boettner, in his explanation of the millennium says, "The world at large will then enjoy a state of righteousness which up until now has been seen only in relatively small and isolated groups: for example, some family circles, and some local church groups and kindred organizations. This does not mean that there will be a time on this earth when every person will be a Christian or that all sin will be abolished. But it does mean that evil in all its many forms eventually will be reduced to negligible proportions, that Christian principles will be the rule, not the exception, and that Christ will return to a truly Christianized world."[7]

The Postmillennialist believes that the Gospel will go into all the world before Christ returns, not merely as a 'witness' to the nations, but as an effective evangelization agent, transforming the hearts and lives of people in the process.

At the end of the millennium of righteousness and peace, however, there will be

---

[7] Boettner, The Meaning of the Millennium: Four Views, pg. 117-118, InterVarsity Press

a short apostasy which will precede Christ's return. That will then be followed by the resurrection and judgement.

The main difference between Amillennialism and Postmillennialism, then, is the starting point, nature, and length of time of the millennium. As noted before, the Amillennialist marks the beginning of the millennium at the first advent of Christ, whereas the Postmillennialist believes it will start sometime during the present age after the world is Christianized.

The Amillennialist sees Christ reigning in heaven through his Church now, while the Postmillennialist sees a Christianized world of righteousness and peace that makes up the millennium. Finally, the Amillennialist sees the thousand years as a purely symbolic period that represents the period between the first and second advents of Christ, while some Postmillennialists believe that the 'thousand years' may, in fact, be literal.

Historic Premillennialism:

As the name suggests, this was the original (or historic) eschatological view of the early church fathers. In saying that, we must qualify it by adding that it was held by all of the church fathers in the first 300 years of the Church who wrote regarding the last days (we will return to this viewpoint in chapter three).

The Historic Premillennial view is also sometimes called 'Covenantal Premillennialism' because it holds in common with Amillennialism and Postmillennialism a view of the eternal covenant regarding salvation (Hebrews 13:20, 21). In other words, all three of these views hold to a form of Covenant Theology.

Covenant Theology is the belief that God has made an everlasting covenant with His people whom He predestined, redeemed, sanctified, and glorified (Romans 8:30). And that it is this covenant which is from everlasting to everlasting, having been ratified through the blood of Jesus Christ.

What all this means is that there has only ever been one plan of salvation and one people of God, from Adam and Eve to the present. Yes, it is true that God's redemptive plan was administered in different ways in the Old Testament as preparatory, instructive, and predictive to the physical manifestation of our Lord and Saviour Jesus Christ. But the way of salvation has always been the same: by grace alone, through faith alone.

The Apostle Paul tells us in Galatians that Christ is the heir to the promises made to Abraham and that we, as Believers, are joint heirs with Christ to those same promises (Galatians 3:13-29). This is very significant, given the later distinction between Israel and the Church which Dispensational Theology tries to identify.

In saying all of this, it must be made clear that Covenantal Theology was an outgrowth of the systematization of biblical theology at the time of the Reformation and was not taught (in this fashion) during the time of the early Church. All of these embryonic covenantal doctrines, however, can be identified in their primitive forms in the writings of the early church fathers.

This is also true regarding the distinctiveness of their prophetic teachings. Here we will give a very brief description of those teachings, as much of this book is devoted to expounding those biblical doctrines in greater detail.

The Historic Premillennial view essentially teaches that, in the last days there will be a great apostasy followed by the rise of a very specific antichrist. This antichrist will be a political leader who will have the power to deceive the nations with the assistance of the false prophet. Along with this there will be a universal persecution of the Church, which will continue to reside on Earth during this horrific period.

During this time (which will last for seven years), God will begin to pour His judgements upon the wicked people of the Earth. There will, however, be a great time of revival as 144,000 Jews become saved (that is, Christians) through the sovereign grace of God. They will begin a worldwide evangelistic campaign the likes of which will eclipse every other evangelical movement in history. As a consequence of their ministry, however, the Beast and the False Prophet will wage war on the Church, creating many Christian martyrs. But these two will meet their end at the battle of Armageddon where they will gather the armies of the nations they have united or subdued under themselves in a cataclysmic (but doomed) stand against Christ.

At this point Christ will return, the resurrection of the Saints will take place, and those who survived the tribulation will be transformed (the so-called 'Rapture') " ... in the twinkling of an eye ... "(1 Corinthians 15:52). The Beast and False Prophet will then be taken and " ... thrown alive into the lake of fire that burns with sulphur" (Revelation 19:20), while their armies will be " … slain by the sword that came from the mouth of Him who was sitting upon the horse (Jesus) … " (Revelation 19:21).

After Armageddon, an angel will then come down and take hold of the devil and imprison him in a 'bottomless pit' (Revelation 20: 1-2) for a thousand years. This will also mark the start of the millennial reign of Christ as King of the Earth along with the first judgement and first resurrection (Revelation 20: 4-5).

After the thousand years expire, however, Satan will be loosed and rally the nations one more time in an attempt to defeat God, again (Revelation 20:7-9). As the Beast and False prophet find out, however, that won't happen, and they will end up sharing their fate in the lake of fire.

Following this, the Great White Throne Judgement will take place (Revelation 20:11). This is the second and final judgement, when all the wicked will be judged and thrown into the lake of fire as well. God will then destroy the old Heaven and Earth and create a new one (Revelation 21:1), ending history and heralding the beginning of eternity with Him (Revelation 21:3).

Dispensational Premillennialism:

Dispensational Premillennialism (or Dispensationalism), is unlike the other three views we have discussed as it does not hold to a Reformed Covenantal view of God's program of redemption. Dispensationalists, instead, have developed a system of biblical interpretation whereby they subdivide the redemptive biblical narrative into seven distinct periods of time. These are:

1) Man in innocence – before the fall;

2) Man under conscience – from the fall until the flood;

3) Man under government – from the fall until the call of Abraham;

4) Man under promise – from the call of Abraham until Moses;

5) Man under law – from Moses to Christ;

6) Man under Grace – from the death and resurrection of Christ until His second coming;

7) Man under the personal reign of Christ – the thousand year Millennium.[8]

According to Dispensational teaching, God has created these 'dispensations of time' to

---

[8] The Word of Truth Rightly Divided, C.I. Scofield, Back to the Bible Publication, pg. 14-18

represent different and distinct periods of testing for mankind. In every dispensation, however, man fails this test and, therefore, God institutes yet another dispensation in order to manage or fine-tune His program of redemption.

This teaching, however, is not the defining factor in Dispensationalism. The real driving force behind this view of prophecy is the centrality of Israel in it.

For Dispensationalists, Israel is biblically huge in God's plan, perhaps equal to the Church itself. It is so big, in fact that they see Israel and the Church as distinct and separate groups, with distinct and separate plans, all ordained by God,[9] an idea we will explore in more detail later in the book.

To Dispensationalists, the Church age is a parenthesis in God's program with Israel. They believe that since the Jews rejected Jesus during His earthly ministry, they essentially forfeited the Kingdom at that point. God then put them aside and is working primarily through the Church, for now.

Eventually, they believe, God will pick up where He left off with Israel after the Church is raptured or 'caught up' and taken away by

---

[9] Ibid, pg. 7-13

Christ before the start of the seven year period of Tribulation. When that happens they think the Holy Spirit of God will be taken away with the Church, too, allowing the Antichrist (or Beast) and the False Prophet to rise and deceive the nations. Additionally they believe that Israel will be persecuted during this period, but God will miraculously save it.

Anyone who is saved during this time, whether they be Jew or Gentile, will be not known as a Christian but as a 'Tribulation Saint,' someone who will be granted the honour of sitting with Christ and rule on Earth when He returns.

At Jesus' return, the False Prophet and the Antichrist will be thrown into the Lake of Fire and Satan will be bound in the Bottomless Pit for the thousand year period. The rule of the Earth will be granted to Israel and all the nations will come to Israel to pay homage to Christ at this time.

Many Dispensationalists also believe that the Old Testament saints will be raised when Jesus returns and rule with Christ, while the Church remains in Heaven. There are, however, some differing perspectives on this.

During the Millennium that follows Christ's return, Dispensationalists believe that the Old Testament temple worship and animal sacrifice will be resumed as a remembrance of Christ's own sacrifice. At the end of the Millennium, Satan will be loosed from his captivity and start another rebellion. This time, however, he will be utterly defeated and cast into the Lake of Fire.

After these events the Great White Throne Judgement occurs and all the wicked will be resurrected and thrown into the Lake of Fire as well. God will then make a New Heaven and New Earth which will usher in eternity.

There is some dispute among Dispensationalists as to whether Israel will then join the Church or not. In fact, if you do the math correctly, there can be as many as four distinct groups of saved people in Dispensational theology; 1) Pre-Abrahamic Saints; 2) Israel; 3) The Church; and 4) Tribulation Saints.

We pray that this quick summation of the four main prophetic interpretations of end-time events has been adequate to give a basic knowledge of the arguments we will present in the course of this book.

Many Christians believe that the study of prophecy is not important and somewhat confusing. We disagree. Yes, there are things in the Bible that are hard to understand, but it doesn't mean we should ignore them either.

We believe that prophecy is put in the Scriptures to give the Believer confidence in the future, to understand that God purposed future events to take place for His glory, that He controls it all, and that it will take place precisely as He determined from the beginning of time (Isaiah 46:9-10).

We also believe that a Believer's interpretation of prophecy will affect and manifest itself in how they respond to a changing world. That said, our understanding of prophecy should not be divorced from the other great doctrines of the faith but rather intertwine and connect with them all, just like all true biblical theology.

Let us pray, therefore, that God will give us wisdom and grace so that we may become receptive to His truth, and grant us grace, through His blessed Holy Spirit, that we may apply all that we might learn.

2

Dispensationalism: Its History, Theology, and Impact

One of the major difficulties with Dispensationalism, developed in the 1830's and which it cannot overcome, is it's a relatively new arrival upon the historical scene. This is despite attempts by people like Charles Ryrie and others, to downplay it.

One method that Dispensationalists use to remove the stigma of the newness of their beliefs is denial. They contend that their system goes back to the earliest days of the Church, even going so far as to identify the Premillennialism of the early Church with Dispensationalism.

In his book, 'Dispensationalism,' Ryrie devotes an entire chapter to trying to prove that there were elements of Dispensationalism in the writings of men from the past. We will address this claim later on, but for now, let us turn to the details of the historicity of Dispensationalism.

As mentioned earlier Dispensationalism began in the 1830's from the mind of British Anglican minister John Nelson Darby (1800-1882). Darby was disillusioned by the current apostasy he saw within the Anglican Church. In the midst of his disillusionment he began to develop a new interpretive approach to understanding the Bible, seeking to reconcile the supposed difficulties he saw between the earthly promises made to the Jews, and the spiritual promises made to the Church. What he developed was the idea that the Bible should be subdivided into seven unequal periods of time which Darby termed 'dispensations.'

The term 'dispensation' does appear in the King James Version of the Scriptures which Darby and Schofield were accustomed to (1 Corinthians 9:17; Ephesians 1:10, 3:2; Colossians 1:25), but never holds the idea of being a 'period of time' as some Dispensationalists would have us to believe. In fact, those words in the English Standard Version are translated as 'stewardship.' C.I. Scofield, however, defined it this way: "A dispensation is a period of time during which man is tested in respect of obedience to some specific revelation of the will of God."[10] He also says that, "under the Mosaic or 'old' dispensation, the gospel was presented in types and shadows, and the Epistle to the Hebrews shows the relation between this former dispensation and that of the gospel ... "[11]

The word Dispensation comes from the Greek word oikonomia, which actually means the "administration (of a household or estate); specially, a (religious) 'economy.'"[12] To give later Dispensationalists credit, they have modified and expanded their definition of dispensation to include the more biblical understanding of the word in regards to stewardship.

Ryrie defines it this way: "A dispensation is a distinguishable economy in the outworking

---

[10] The New Scofield Study Bible, pg. 3, note 3, 1967

[11] Ibid., pg. 168

[12] Strong's Exhaustive Concordance Of The Bible, Riverside Book and Bible House, Iowa Falls, Iowa

of God's purpose."[13] They do, however, retain their ideas that 1) man is accountable within the dispensation to secure success, 2) unfaithfulness may result in a change of the administration/dispensation, and 3) a dispensation can come to an end at any time.[14] All of this implies that the original Dispensationalist idea that man's failure in the specific dispensations results in God changing His program. Ryrie says that in describing a dispensation he would, " ... include other things such as the ideas of distinctive revelation, responsibility, testing, failure, and judgement." [15]

The main issue, however, is that Darby perceived a genuine demarcation between the Church and Israel in Scripture. This, incidentally, is what the whole system of Dispensational thought is built upon; the pillar or main beam upon which his whole construct rests and is supported by. This idea will be discussed in more detail in chapter seven.

Shortly after his disillusionment with the Anglican Church Darby became associated with

---

[13] Dispensationalism, Charles Ryrie, pg. 28

[14] Ibid., chapter 2

[15] Ibid., pg. 28

the Brethren Movement, which began in the late 1820's. The Brethren—Plymouth Brethren as they were then known—originated in Dublin, Ireland, and Plymouth, England, by founders Edward Cronin, John Bellett, and Francis Hutchinson in response to concerns about the spiritual condition of the National (or Anglican) Church. Their main distinctiveness was in having no ordained ministers (they emphasized equality and unity among their members), and an ecumenical spirit which allowed anyone, from any denomination, to have fellowship with them.

At that time in history, these were considered quite radical and progressive ideas. But as their congregations grew, the Brethren also discovered these ideals also created significant problems too.

By not having any formal (or ordained) clergy or ministers, it was the ones with the strongest personalities who quickly became leaders in the movement. Darby was one of these men, and it was not long before his doctrines began permeating throughout the movement; so much so that, even now, Dispensationalism and the Brethren movement are virtually synonymous.

By the latter part of the 1800's Darby's teachings had jumped the pond and were being spread throughout North America; largely through the efforts of a man named James Inglis (1813-1872) via his monthly magazine called 'Waymarks in the Wilderness' which was published intermittently between 1854 and 1872. The continuing spread of this doctrine eventually led to The Niagara Conferences, which were held annually between the years 1876 to 1897 at Niagara-On-The-Lake, Ontario.

James H. Brookes (1830-1898), a pastor in St. Louis, Missouri, organized these conferences, the main purpose of which was to teach and promote the prophetic views of this new system of theology. This culminated in the 1878 document of faith known as the "Niagara Creed," a fourteen point statement that was one of the first to explicitly proclaim a faith in the premillennial return of Jesus.[16]

The interesting thing about the Creed was that it does not explicitly affirm Dispensationalism, though it does refer to many of its beliefs, such as the restoration of Israel and

---

[16] https://en.wikipedia.org/wiki/Niagara_Bible_Conference

millennial period.[17] Eventually, however, the conferences ended. Ironically this was because not everyone who took part in them could accept the Pretribulation Rapture; something the Dispensationalists among them felt so strongly about that the controversy was the major factor which led to the decline and eventual demise of the conferences.[18]

From these conferences, however, and their ecumenical nature, Dispensationalism firmly took root in many denominations and the leading lights of the period, such as D.L. Moody and his Moody Bible Institute (founded in 1886). It was further popularized and brought into the mainstream by C.I. Scofield in his famed Scofield Reference Bible (first published in 1909).

Dr. Lewis Sperry Chaffer, an associate of Scofield's (he would help him set up the Philadelphia School of the Bible, later serving there as a Bible lecturer from 1914-1922),[19] also played a key role in the spread of Dispensational ideas. He, along with his friend and fellow

---

[17] https://en.wikipedia.org/wiki/Niagara_Bible_Conference

[18] In Pursuit of Purity: American Fundamentalism Since 1850, David O. Beale, pg. 28, 29

[19] https://www.theopedia.com/lewis-sperry-chafer

pastor William Henry Griffith Thomas, would go on to found the Dallas Theological Seminary in 1924. This institution quickly grew into the largest Protestant theological seminary of its time, and has been a major influence in training up men for the ministry; men who would spread Dispensationalism into ever more churches in North America.

As a result of these key historical figures and events, the Pretribulation Rapture is the leading (though not the majority) prophetic doctrine of churches in North America in our day. According to the website, Christianity Today, as much as 36% of Protestant pastors believe in the PreTrib Rapture.[20] This would not be possible were it not for the spread of Dispensationalism, which is the driving force behind the Pretribulation Rapture theory, without which it could not exist. And although Dispensationalists firmly believe it to be a 'literal interpretation' of Scripture, the truth is that they have it only partially correct—it is only an 'interpretation,' but one riddled with serious scriptural and doctrinal inconsistencies. This claim is discussed in full in chapter 6.

---

[20] http://www.christianitytoday.com/news/2016/april/sorry-left-behind-pastors-end-times-rapture-antichrist.html

As we said earlier, Dispensational theology divides Scripture into seven distinct periods that it asserts are clearly defined in the Bible: Man Innocent, Man under Conscience, Man in Authority over the Earth, Man under Promise, Man under Law, Man under Grace, and Man under the Personal Reign of Christ.[21] A necessary requirement to these seven distinct periods is a different end-times program between Israel and the Church. As we already said, it is this distinction that is critical to making the whole system work.

We cannot emphasize this enough. The Dispensationalist has to view every biblical interpretation they come to through the prism of whether a particular Scripture refers to Israel or the Church. This difference is also central to the Pretrib Rapture doctrine. Not only does Dispensationalism fail their self-administered 'literalism' test, but it also makes the body of their views untenable.

The Pretribulation Rapture doctrine can only exist within this theological framework. Dwight Pentecost, a Dispensational theologian, stated in his book, 'Things to Come,'

---

[21] Taken from, The Word of Truth Rightly Divided, C.I. Scofield

"Pretribulation rapturism rests essentially on one major premise—the literal method of interpretation of the Scriptures. As a necessary adjunct to this, the pretribulationalist believes in a dispensational interpretation of the Word of God."[22] In other words, to believe in a Pretribulation Rapture of the Church you not only have to accept Dispensationalism, but you must also believe that this system has a monopoly on the literal interpretation of Scripture.

This assertion is misguided, yet it has been widely accepted as fact by many of the Evangelical Protestant congregations and denominations in North America today. This is also the reason why so many Christians (who have been taught this literally from the first time they go to church) are so reluctant to give up their Dispensation-based ideas. Many think that if they do then they will, of necessity, have to interpret all of the Bible allegorically and potentially drift into liberalism.

The intriguing part about Pentecost's assertion that Dispensationalists are the only ones who interpret the Bible literally is that he

---

[22] J. Dwight Pentecost, Things To Come: A Study in Biblical Eschatology, pg. 193

holds up two of the greatest men of the Reformation, Luther and Calvin, to support his position. This completely ignores the fact that both these men, who also advocated a literal interpretation of Scripture, were not Pretribulational or even Premillennial—they were Amillennial.

Pentecost writes: "The foundations of the Reformation were laid in the return to the literal method of interpretation. In the Reformation period itself two great names stand out as exponents of the truths of Scripture: Luther and Calvin. Both of these are marked by their strong (insistence) on the literal method of interpretation."[23] Both Luther and Calvin were tremendous champions of the faith. These great teachers, along with others far too numerous to mention here, helped bring an end to the Dark Age of Roman Catholic domination of Christendom, and brought back the rediscovered doctrines of the Gospel.

Luther and Calvin, however, thoroughly and completely contradict Pentecost's belief that Dispensationalists are the only literal exegetes, due to their Amillennialism. That Pentecost does not comprehend this demonstrates either a

---

[23] Ibid., J. Dwight Pentecost, pg. 27

profound misunderstanding of these Reformers, or (God forbid) a deliberate misrepresentation on his part.

Dispensationalists also believe that Pretribulationism was actually held by the early Church, and that Darby was simply reaffirming it. Pentecost says, "The Early Church lived in the light of the imminent return of Christ. Their expectation was that Christ might return at any time. Pretribulationalism is the only position consistent with this doctrine of imminence."[24] In other words, on one hand Pentecost says you need a Dispensational position in order to believe in the Pretrib Rapture (based on a 'literal interpretation' of Scripture), and on the other that the early Church was Pretribulational; which is impossible given the fact that Dispensationalism can only be traced back to the 1830's!

George Eldon Ladd (1911-1982), Baptist minister and professor at the Fuller Theological Seminary in Pasadena, California, backs this up further. He stated that though, indeed, the early Church was Premillennial, the prophetic program being taught today (Dispensationalism), " ... included important

---

[24] Ibid., J. Dwight Pentecost, pg. 166

elements which are not found in the early church. Among these were the teachings of the rapture of the Church at the beginning of the tribulation and the expectation of an any-moment secret coming of Christ for the purpose of rapturing the Church."[25]

In our experience many honest Bible-believing Christians have not heard, know, or even understand what Dispensationalism is, along with its relatively recent theological origin. However, they invariably accept most of the doctrines disseminated from it. The reason for this is that many Pastors are themselves, offspring of a Bible school or Seminary in which this system of theology is taught, and also where a serious examination of Darby's theology is likely not even considered.

Many have probably never even heard of Darby, nor appreciate just how powerful an influence his teachings have had on the theological training they had or are still receiving. In addition to this, it is interesting to note that Dispensationalists have been, and are, very prolific writers, especially in the realm of prophecy, thus further spreading his ideas.

---

[25] George Eldon Ladd, The Blessed Hope, pg. 8

This leads us to the next, and probably best known, means of spreading Dispensationalism throughout the Church, the fascination many people have with the New York Times best-selling 'Left Behind' books by Tim LaHaye and Jerry B. Jenkins. These novels, which have sold tens of millions of copies, and also spawned several movies, are set in the present era and represent a fictionalized expression of the events in the Revelation of John after the supposed Pretribulation Rapture has taken place.

Set against the backdrop of the Great Tribulation, in which the Christian church and believers have been raptured, these books and movies are filled with interesting and sympathetic characters, who are forced to face the coming onslaught of the antichrist and the one-world system that begins to dominate this period. They also provide LaHaye and Jenkins the perfect vehicle through which to promote and disseminate Dispensational thinking to the masses in ways Darby could only dream of.

In order to further defend and expound Pretribulationism, Tim LaHaye, along with Thomas Ice, founded the Pretribulation Research Center (PTRC) in 1993, which is composed of over 200 so-called 'prophecy scholars.' To date, the PTRC has produced an impressive volume of literature in defence of the Pretribulation Rapture, reinforcing their views in the minds of many Christians. The trouble is that, instead of teaching people how to think, they are teaching them what to think.

In short, what the PTRC does not teach is how to question the Dispensationalism itself, or how it stands when critiqued by the Scriptures themselves. Since the validity of their ideology is considered beyond question, its conclusions must also be inerrant and those who oppose, or even challenge them, are severely uniformed or troublemakers.

That appears, in our own experience, to be the prevailing attitude when one raises doubts or demands Bible-based answers regarding Dispensational supposition, including the Pre-Trib Ratpure. The unfortunate thing about this is that, instead of encouraging people to individually come to a sound understanding of eschatology and true biblical prophecy through a vigorous study of Scripture, you more or less need a supposed 'prophecy expert' to teach it to you.

This has gotten so bad, in fact, that some of these 'experts' are considered to be prophetic 'giants;' men uniquely gifted to expound biblical prophecy. Even Tim LaHaye is not immune from doing this. In speaking of Dr. John Walvoord in his book 'The Rapture: Who Will Face the Tribulation,' LaHaye calls him, "the dean of all living prophecy scholars and authors!"[26]

This said, we are not denying that there are, indeed, preachers and teachers in the Church who were gifted and placed there by God in order to instruct and edify the Body of Christ. We ourselves appreciate the writings of the Reformers, Puritans, and many others who have followed in that great lineage. But to believe, however, that these 'prophecy scholars' possess a special anointing or gift which uniquely qualifies them to expound a certain Biblical theme, seems wrong indeed.

As Christians we are encouraged to seek wisdom and discern between truth and error (1 John 4:1) in order to show ourselves approved unto God (2 Timothy 2:15). The reason so many false doctrines have crept into the Church, and will continue to do so, is because Christians are allowing corrupt doctrines to flourish like weeds and choke off biblical truth and sound doctrine.

---

[26] Tim LaHaye, The Rapture: Who Will Face the Tribulation? pg. 11

There is no harm in sincerely questioning what you have been taught, especially if it comes from genuine desire to know what the truth is. Nor is it wrong to lean and wait upon God to reveal it to you because, in the end, truth and error become always self-evident in the light of Scripture.

The problem today is that many ministers are just as undiscerning as those whom they teach. They are either reluctant, or unwilling, to question the system of theology which feeds their interpretation of Scripture. Some, we are convinced, either do not know they are teaching a system rather than the literal Bible, or have never thought to question it.

The reason for this, as we see it, is because many people, ministers and laity alike, are simply lazy. They would rather, it seems to us, have someone else spoon-feed them God's Word instead of exploring its riches for themselves.

Please understand that we are not here to cast down the writings of eminent men in the Church who have produced great commentaries, books on specific doctrines, etc. which are incredibly useful. We are merely saying that even these have to be brought under the scrutiny of Scripture.

If what they write has been found, by your examination, to be the truth, then hold onto it and cherish it. But on the other hand you must also be ready to abandon an error whenever you encounter it.

A simple way to keep this in mind is to remember that whenever you read a commentary or exposition *about* the Scriptures (or any subject for that matter), *you* sit in judgement over that work. But when you read the Bible, ***it sits in judgement over you!***

The Apostle Paul commands believers to "Let the word of Christ dwell in you richly, teaching and admonishing one another in all wisdom … " (Colossians 3:16). In other words, Christians are to let the Scriptures saturate their entire lives "in all wisdom" so that they understand and obey that which they read.

Earlier we made the observation that the Dispensational system came to flourish in the United States and Canada, and we traced, briefly, how this came to be. These two countries are the real bastions for Dispensational theology. If you were to travel to the British Isles, Europe, or anywhere else in the world, however, you would be hard pressed to attend a 'prophecy conference,' although they are heavily promoted among many North American Evangelical churches.

Combined with seminaries, preachers, books, and prophecy conferences, it is only natural that the Dispensational Pre-trib Rapture doctrine should come to have a stranglehold on Premillennialist thinking.

3

The Historical Record: The Roots of the Eschatological Divide

Within Protestant Reformed Christianity it is not uncommon for us to examine the past in order to understand what the great Christian men of those eras taught and believed. This is not done because these men are somehow considered to be infallible. We simply realize that the Holy Spirit of God used them, in their time, to expound the truth of the Word of God.[27] In doing this we see numerous common threads (many times in their infancy) of the same great doctrines we hold to today. Furthermore, by examining their writings, we can gain an insight into the times they lived in, and understand how some early church doctrines were taught and defended in their times.

Some Dispensationalists like to claim that the Bible is their authority, not history. While we, also, affirm this, the implication is that anyone who refers to Church history must, of necessity, be using it as their primary authority and not the Scriptures. This is not true.

Church history is not the authoritative rule for faith and practice as the Word of God is, it is merely a guide. George Eldon Ladd, Professor of New Testament Exegesis and Theology at Fuller Theological Seminary in

---

[27] Ephesians 4:8-13 teaches us that this is indeed the case. In this text the Apostle tells us that gifted men are given to the Church to bring her to maturity, and that this work will continue until it is brought unto "the measure of the stature of the fullness of Christ" (vs. 13). We understand this to mean that throughout history there have been men, placed there by God, that continue the work of edifying the body of Christ, and delving deeper into the doctrines which were delivered to her. There are no new doctrines since that time, but a deeper and more mature understanding of the truths which have been given to us.

Pasadena, California (1950-1980) explained this well, saying, "Let it be at once emphasized that we are not turning to the church fathers to find authority for either pre or post tribulationism. The one authority is the Word of God, and we are not confined in the straitjacket of tradition ... While tradition does not provide authority, it would nevertheless be difficult to suppose that God had left His people in ignorance of an essential truth for nineteen centuries."[28]

Phillip Schaff, church historian and Protestant theologian (1819-1893) says, "Nothing is more characteristic of radicalism and sectarianism than an utter want of historical sense and respect for the past."[29] And the Scriptures itself says, " ... whatever was written in former days was written for our instruction, that through endurance and through the encouragement of the Scriptures we might have hope" (Romans 15:4). While this text specifically speaks about the Old Testament Scriptures, we believe that it has an application in the realm of church history; a lesson that is often ignored at our peril.

---

[28] George Eldon Ladd, The Blessed Hope, Pg. 19-20.

[29] Schaff, History of the Christian Church, Vol. 8, pg. 71

We do not want to disseminate false doctrines. If a teaching or a doctrine is relatively new, such as Dispensationalism and the Pre-Trib Rapture, then one has to wonder how the early disciples and church fathers missed it. And if those closest to the Apostles, who learned and gleaned from them in person or were only a couple of generations removed from them, never held to the views now being widely spread, the question should rightly be asked is why?

When viewing church history, we observe that a lot of the theological terms we have today were developed and instituted as the church began to grow. Terms such as: Trinity, Hypostasis, Soteriology, Christology, etc., were not around at the founding of the church, but were developed later on as the need arose for the Church to declare their doctrines more clearly.

This is not a problem. In fact, a careful study of church history reveals that the roots of present terms find expression in teachings from the earliest church fathers, and are grounded in sound Scriptural exegesis. In saying that, we must also state that we do not want to give the reader the impression that the early Church fathers were completely unanimous and sound in all that they taught.

Even some of the greatest teachers, such as Augustine, who proclaimed much sound biblical truth, also taught certain doctrines which were in error.[30] The Church Fathers then have to be read with discernment and care to ascertain the truth from the Word. Red flags are raised, however, only when no record can be found in their writings of a certain doctrine, even in its infancy.

In the last chapter we mentioned Charles Ryrie's claim that Dispensational teaching can be found in some of the writings of the men from the past. Chapter 4 of his book, 'Dispensationalism,' is in fact dedicated to this very subject. In it he quotes Justin Martin (110-165), Irenaeus (130-200), Augustine (354-430), Pierre Poiret (1646-1719), John Edwards (1637-1716 — this is not Jonathan Edwards, the great Puritan preacher of New England during the Great Awakening), and Isaac

---

[30] For example, he, as many of the early Church teachers did in his time, exalted monasticism. He also postulated the possibility of purgatory, and taught the sinless birth and life of Mary, but did not, however, teach the Immaculate Conception. For this last point see Schaff, History of the Christian Church, vol. 3, pg. 418, 419, Hendrickson Publishers. See also Nicene and Post Nicene Fathers, vol. 5, Augustine: Anti-Pelagian Writings, pg. 135, chapter 42, Hendrickson Publishers.

Watts (1674-1748) in support of his views. But when you look more closely at the evidence Ryrie provides, you will see that the main distinctive of Dispensationalism (the separation, and differing programs, between Israel and the Church) is conspicuously absent.

Now if you want to break up the Bible into historical sections, to more easily understand the flow, there is no problem. But if, as the Dispensationalists do, you see a different divine program for Israel and the Church, claim certain passages of Scripture which are for Israel and certain ones that are for the Church, teach a Pre-Trib Rapture, and a whole host of other Dispensational distinctiveness, there really is a problem.

In doing his survey of history, Ryrie does not prove one of these distinctive doctrines, thus further ensuring in our minds the knowledge that these ideas were developed in the 19th century by Darby and those who followed his teaching. In fact, when Ryrie quotes the small passage from Justin Martyr, he completely disregards the context and the rest of Justin's book!

Ryrie says, "Justin Martyr (110-165) held a concept of differing programs of God. In the 'Dialogue with Trypho,' while discussing the subject that God always taught the same righteousness, he said, "If one should wish to ask you why, since Enoch, Noah with his sons, and all others in similar circumstances, who neither were circumcised nor kept the Sabbath, pleased God, God demanded by other leaders and by the giving of the law after the lapse of so many generations, that those who lived between the times of Abraham and of Moses be justified by circumcision and the other ordinances—to wit, the Sabbath, and sacrifices, and libation, and offerings ... (XCII)"[31]

Left at this you would indeed suspect that Justin did teach a different program of Salvation in the Old Testament than in the New. But Justin goes on to say, " ... [God will be slandered] unless you show, as I have already said, that God who foreknew was aware that your nation would deserve expulsion from Jerusalem, and that none would be permitted to enter into it. For you are not distinguished in any other way than by the fleshly circumcision, as I remarked previously. For Abraham was declared by God to be righteous, not on account of circumcision, but on account of faith ... And we, therefore, in the uncircumcision of our flesh, believing God

---

[31] Charles Ryrie, Dispensationalism, pg. 63.

through Christ, and having that circumcision ... of the heart—we hope to appear righteous before and well-pleasing to God ... "[32]

Read that again. Justin is saying, forthrightly, that God would be "slandered" if anyone indeed claimed there were differing programs of salvation, and did not explain the reason for the ordinances, sacrifices and libations.

This is further affirmed by rest of his 'Dialogue with Trypho,' which flatly contradicts many Dispensational teachings. For example Justin says, " ... For the true spiritual Israel, and descendants of Judah, Jacob, Isaac, and Abraham ... are we who have been led to God through this crucified Christ ... "[33]

In speaking of the inheritance, Dispensationalists claim that Israel will have their earthly portion and the Church will have their heavenly portion. However, it is recorded in the Dialogue, "And Trypho remarked, 'What is this you say? That none of us shall inherit anything on the holy mountain of God?' And I replied, 'I do not say so; but those who have

---

[32] Ante-Nicene Fathers, Vol. 1, Justin Martyr, Dialogue with Trypho, Chap. XCII, pg. 245.

[33] Ibid. Chap. XI, pg. 200.

persecuted and do persecute Christ, if they do not repent, shall not inherit anything on the holy mountain. But the Gentiles, who have believed on Him, and have repented of the sins which they have committed, they shall receive the inheritance along with the patriarchs and the prophets, and the just men who are descended from Jacob ... "[34] At another place Justin says, "And you deceive yourselves while you fancy that, because you are the seed of Abraham after the flesh, therefore you shall fully inherit the good things announced to be bestowed by God through Christ. For no one, not even of them, has anything to look for, but only those who in mind are assimilated to the faith of Abraham ..."[35]

While speaking on the resurrection, Justin makes it clear that he taught a resurrection of all saints, from all time, at the same moment, which is opposed to the Dispensationalists view of multiple people of God each having distinct resurrections: "Since those who did that which is universally, naturally, and eternally good are pleasing to God, they shall be saved through this

---

[34] Ibid. Chap. XXV. pg. 207

[35] Ibid. Chap. XLIV. pg. 216

Christ in the resurrection equally with those righteous men who were before them, namely Noah, and Enoch, and Jacob, and whoever else there be, along with those who have known this Christ, Son of God ... "[36]

Finally, in a rebuke to Dispensationalists claim that certain portions of the Word of God do not belong to the Church (such as major portions of the writings of the prophets and the Gospels), we see that Justin critically differs from this view. He said to Trypho, "For these words have neither been prepared by me, nor embellished by the art of man; but David sung them, Isaiah preached them, Zechariah proclaimed them, and Moses wrote them. Are you acquainted with them, Trypho? They are contained in your Scriptures, or rather ***not yours, but ours*** (emphasis ours)."[37]

There are many more quotations which we could pull out of Justin's Dialogue, but time and space does not permit us to. But from these, alone, it is clear that Ryrie completely took his "proof" way out of context.

---

[36] Ibid. Chap. XLV. pg. 217

[37] Ibid. Chap. XXIX, pg. 209

As for the rest of the people whom Ryrie quotes (and as we already noted), they all mention in their writings a timeline of dispensations or economies. This, as we said, does not make you Dispensational. It is the proposed separation between Israel and the Church that the Dispensationalists hold to that makes one Dispensational.

Even Ryrie admits this when he says, "The essence of Dispensationalism, then, is the distinction between Israel and the church."[38] Ryrie then claims that this distinction is made from a literal interpretation of the Bible: "This grows out of the Dispensationalists' consistent employment of the normal or plain or historical-grammatical interpretation, and it reflects an understanding of the basic purpose of God in all His dealings with mankind as that of glorifying Himself through salvation and other purposes as well."[39] As already mentioned, we will dispel this idea of the Dispensationalists' claim to be literal in their interpretation, and show rather how their system drives their interpretation instead of having it arise out of the text.

---

[38] Charles Ryrie, Dispensationalism, pg. 41.

[39] Ibid.

One will search in vain throughout the pages of church history (with the exception of Darby) to find any distinction between Israel and the Church, which is the foundation of this theology. The claims which Ryrie attests, that "… there are historical references to that which eventually was systematized into dispensationalism. There is evidence in the writings of men who lived long before Darby that the dispensational concept was a part of their viewpoint,"[40] is misleading.

Yes there is talk of time periods and even Dispensations in some writings but this, as we must stress again, does not make one Dispensational. The distinction between Israel and the Church is the component which makes one a Dispensationalist, and the one which is conspicuously absent.

Now concerning the early churches and their understanding of the timing of the Resurrection, history has provided us a glimpse into the theological position many of them espoused. Schaff, for example, says, "The most striking point in the eschatology of the ante-Nicene age (A.D. 100-325) is the prominent

---

[40] Ibid. pg. 63.

chiliasm[41], or millennarianism, that is the belief of a visible reign of Christ in glory on earth with the risen saints for a thousand years, before the general resurrection and judgement. It was indeed not the doctrine of the church embodied in any creed or form of devotion, but a widely current opinion of distinguished teachers, such as Barnabas, Papias, Justin Martyr, Irenaeus, Tertullian, Methodius, and Lactantius ... "[42]

Here's what some of these men believed: Justin Martyr wrote, " ... O unreasoning men! understanding not what has been proved by all these passages, that two advents of Christ has been announced: the one, in which He is set forth as suffering, inglorious, dishonored, and crucified; but the other, in which He shall come from heaven with glory, when the man of apostasy, who speaks strange things against the Most High, shall venture to do unlawful deeds on the earth against us the Christians, who,

---

[41] Chiliasm ... is the Greek millenarianism or millennialism (from mille anni), the Latin term for the same theory. The adherents are called Chiliasts, or Millennarians, also Pre-millennarians, or Premillennialists ... , Schaff, History of the Christian Church, Vol. 2, pg. 614, footnote 1, Hendrickson Publishers

[42] Schaff, History of the Christian Church, Vol. 2, pg. 614, Hendrickson Publishers.

having learned the true worship of God from the law, and the word which went forth from Jerusalem by means of the apostles of Jesus, have fled for safety to the God of Jacob and God of Israel ... "[43]

Justin lived at a time when Rome was the dominant power in the world. The Jewish nation had been utterly destroyed, while Christians lived with the knowledge that, one day, they might have to lay down their lives for the faith. Justin himself was later murdered for his witness and yet even he, during this terrible time, believed that Christians would, at some future time, still face persecution by the Man of Apostasy, the Man of Sin, aka the Antichrist.

This is Post-Tribulation, not Dispensational Pre-Tribulation theology. If, as the Dispensationalists claim, the early church espoused their views and that their views are derived from Scripture, Justin himself never knew it or shared it.

Another early church father who believed that the Church was to be persecuted by the Antichrist, and who wrote abundantly concerning the end times, was Hippolytus. This

---

[43] Ante-Nicene Fathers, Vol. 1, Justin Martyr, Dialogue with Trypho, Chap. CX, pg. 253-254.

saint of God was of Greek origin and a Bishop of Rome from the latter part of the second century until the early part of the third (A.D. 170-236). In his writings on Christ's coming he says, "Now, concerning the tribulation of the persecution which is to fall upon the Church from the adversary, John also speaks thus: 'And I saw a great and wondrous sign in heaven; a woman clothed with the sun ... And to the woman were given two wings of the great eagle, that she might fly into the wilderness, where she is nourished for a time, times, and half a time, from the face of the serpent.' That refers to the one thousand two hundred and three score days (the half of the week) during which the tyrant is to reign and persecute the Church ... "[44]

Notice, again, that Hippolytus foresees the persecution of the Church at the hands of the Antichrist, not its escape from it! If, as the Dispensationalists claim, they merely espouse the historical view held by the early church, it was a position that Hippolytus, like Justin, never knew about. The same was true of Irenaeus, Hippolytus' teacher.

---

[44] Ante-Nicene Fathers, Vol. 5, pg. 217, Hippolytus, Treatise on Christ and Antichrist, 60-61.

Irenaeus (A.D. 120-202) was the Bishop of Lyons and a man mightily used of God in the defence of the faith. He was, in turn, a disciple of Polycarp, who was himself a disciple of the Apostle John. Schaff even notes this when he writes, "Irenaeus, on the strength of tradition from St. John and his disciples, taught that after the destruction of the Roman empire, and the brief raging of antichrist (lasting three and a half years or 1260 days), Christ will visibly appear, will bind Satan, will reign at the rebuilt city of Jerusalem ... "[45] While this doesn't prove that the Post-Trib view is correct, it, nonetheless, adds credibility to that view due to their direct link to the author of the book of the Revelation himself.

During Irenaeus's life heresies abounded and spread abroad everywhere. It was at this time that he began his vigorous defence of the faith. Fortunately, many of his writings were preserved and, because of that, we have access to his insights about many of the doctrines of the Church in the second century.

Concerning Christ's return, Irenaeus says, "For He (Christ) came to divide a man against his father, and the daughter against the mother,

---

[45] Schaff, History of the Christian Church, Vol. 2, pg. 617.

and the daughter-in-law against the mother in-law; and when two are in one bed, to take the one and leave the other; and of two women grinding at the mill, to take one and leave the other: [also] at the time of the end, to order the reapers to collect first the tares together, and bind them in bundles, and burn them with unquenchable fire, but to gather up the wheat into the barn; and to call the lambs into the kingdom prepared for them, but to send the goats into everlasting fire ... the chaff, indeed, which is the apostasy, being cast away; but the wheat, that is, those who bring forth fruit to God in faith, being gathered into the barn. And for this cause tribulation is necessary for those who are saved, that having been after a manner broken up, and rendered fine, and sprinkled over by the patience of the Word of God, and set on fire [for purification], they may be fitted for the royal banquet."[46]

Irenaeus believed, unlike Dispensationalists do today, that the Church has to go through this time of trial so that she might be purified. What is interesting is that, at the time of his writing, the Church had already

---

[46] Ante-Nicene Fathers, Vol. 1, pg. 556-557, Irenaeus, Against Heresies, Book V, Chap. XXVII. 1. & XXVIII. 4.

endured much persecution at the hands of the Jews and Romans.

Irenaeus actually bore witness to the purification of the saints as they were martyred for their faith in Christ. He is even credited with the writing of the account of the holy martyrs in which Justin Martyr and his friends were murdered.

Interestingly Irenaeus and others did not believe that they were somehow going to evade the final persecution to come but that God had, in fact, ordained it according to the Scriptures. Because of that, they were willing to accept all kinds of evil for the sake of their faith in Christ, and not be dissuaded by the terrible price that it would exact in terms of their lives and their liberty.

As the Bible says, " ... they loved not their lives even unto death" (Revelation 12:11). They, like Moses, chose " ... rather to be mistreated with the people of God than to enjoy the fleeting pleasures of sin. He considered the reproach of Christ greater wealth than the treasures of Egypt, for he was looking to the reward" (Hebrews 11:25, 26).

These were some of the earliest pastors and teachers of the Church after the Apostles of Christ themselves, and it is a historic fact that many of them bore witness to the belief of a Post-Tribulation return of Jesus Christ. After the first few centuries of church history, however, the idea of a future Antichrist, along with a period of intense tribulation, followed by the return of Christ to set up a thousand year kingdom, gradually disappeared.

Augustine played a key role in this, bringing into the church the teaching of Amillennialism, which eventually represented the dominant view from about the fourth century onward. Ladd says, "During the Middle Ages, the 'historical' interpretation of Revelation arose in which the book was thought to give in symbolic form an outline of the history of the Church. Antichrist was frequently interpreted to mean the Saracens, and the false prophet to mean Mohammed. Pope Innocent III made effective use of the Revelation to stir up support for his crusade."[47]

Another factor that led to the rise of Amillennialism was the change of the social condition of the Church during the 4th century. Almost overnight the Church went from an oppressed religious sect, outlawed and persecuted, to having acceptance and

---

[47] George Eldon Ladd, The Blessed Hope, Pg. 31.

acknowledgement of its rights from the state, with Constantine's assumption of power and supposed conversion (circa. 312).

During the Ante-Nicene age, the Church, with its many struggles in this world, looked forward with anticipation to the return of Christ and the Millennial Kingdom, which were taught in the Scriptures. Thus, with the persecution of Christians and the Christian church abated under the reign of Constantine, the Church became comfortable with its new found position in the world. Schaff writes, "But the crushing blow (that of Premillennialism) came from the great change in the social condition and prospects of the church in the Nicene age. After Christianity, contrary to all expectation, triumphed in the Roman empire, and was embraced by the Caesars themselves, the millennial reign, instead of being anxiously waited and prayed for, began to be dated either from the first appearance of Christ, or from the conversion of Constantine and the downfall of paganism, and to be regarded as realized in the glory of the dominant imperial state-church. Augustine, who himself had formerly entertained chiliastic hopes, framed the new theory which reflected the social change, and was generally accepted."[48]

In the writings of the men at the time of the Reformation in the 16th century and onward, we see that, they too, accepted this type of historical interpretation of Revelation, and end time prophecy. Luther said he actually despised the book of the Revelation when he issued the first introduction to it in his German translation of 1522. He said, "About this book of the Revelation of John, I leave everyone free to hold his own opinions. I would not have anyone bound to my opinion or judgement. I say what I feel. I miss more than one thing in this book, and it makes me consider it to be neither apostolic nor prophetic ... I can in no way detect that the Holy Spirit produced it."[49]

By 1530, however, Luther had reversed his opinion, and in all subsequent editions of the New Testament, including his complete translation of the Bible in 1545, he wrote a new and expanded preface, a portion of which states, "There are many different kinds of prophecy in Christendom. One is prophecy which interprets

---

[48] Schaff, History of the Christian Church, Vol. 2, pg. 619.

[49] Martin Luther, Luther's Works, Word and Sacrament I, Volume 35, Pg. 398.

the writings of the prophets. Paul speaks of this in I Corinthians 12 and 14, and in other places as well. This is the most necessary kind and we must have it every day, because it teaches the Word of God, lays the foundation of Christendom and defends the faith. In a word, it rules, preserves, establishes, and performs the preaching ministry. Another kind foretells things to come which are not previously contained in Scripture, and this prophecy is of three types. The first expresses itself simply in words, without images and figures … The second type does this with images, but alongside them it supplies their interpretation in specific words … The third type does it without either words or interpretation, exclusively with images and figures, like this book of Revelation … This is the way it has been with this book heretofore … "[50]

Luther then explains Revelation using this historical (more accurately known as historicist) type of interpretation by claiming that the book really explains the entire history of the Church, with the Pope identified as being the Antichrist. This is the standard Amillennial position, as espoused by Augustine (please note that in his time, however, there was no Pope to be

---

[50] Ibid. pg. 399-400.

identified as the Antichrist) and which many Reformers, and Post Reformers, have followed since.

Kim Riddlebarger, in his book 'A Case for Amillennialism,' confirms the origin of this position from the days of Augustine. He says, "In point of fact it is the amillennial position that has been the predominant eschatological view of Christianity since the days of Augustine ... "[51]

In 1706 a man named Daniel Whitby developed a new prophetic view. He taught that the world was to be completely evangelized first, followed by the Millennium in which the Church reigns on the earth until Christ's return. This became known as Postmillennialism. Ladd wrote that this view " ... followed the historical interpretation for the first nineteen chapters (of Revelation) and interpreted the first part of chapter twenty as a future era when the Church would reign over the world after the destruction of anti-Christian Rome."[52]

All of this testifies to the fact that the earliest view held by many in the Church was Premillennialism, with Post-Tribulation Rapture.

---

[51] Kim Riddlebarger, A Case for Amillennialism: Understanding the End Times, Pg. 31

[52] George Eldon Ladd, The Blessed Hope, Pg. 33.

This became known as 'Historic Premillenialism.'[53]

By the fourth century A.D., through Augustine's endeavors and the new relationship between the Church and the Roman Empire, Amillennialism was made the orthodox view, and Premillennialism was condemned as heresy.[54] Then Daniel Whitby came on the scene, and developed Postmillennialism.

This view shared the stage with Amillennialism in the post Reformation, and even today among many in the Reformed tradition as both interpretations share many common facets. Then Darby shows up in the 1830's with the doctrine of Dispensational Premillennialism, which has now become, after 180 years, the prominent eschatological position of the Protestant Evangelical Church in North America.

---

[53] Even the name 'Historic Premillennialism' is conceded by our Dispensational opponents, which says volumes to the validity of this historic view.

[54] Schaff made this plain when he wrote: "From the time of Constantine and Augustin chiliasm took its place among the heresies, and was rejected subsequently even by the Protestant reformers as a Jewish dream." History of the Christian Church, pg. 619. See also his footnote on the same page where he quotes the Augsburg Confession and the 41st article of the Anglican Church.

These are historical facts. But that alone does not mean they are a substitute for sound doctrine, nor do they prove whose eschatology is correct. They do, however, point to the original position of the early Church (Historic Premillennialism) and show how, over time, that foundation was buried eventually by these other prophetic views.

Our hope is that we have refuted the unsupportable claims by Dispensationalists who believe their position is that of the early Church. The historical record, in fact, bears this out. To suggest otherwise contradicts the documented evidence.

4

The Pre-Trib Rapture: Preaching Salvation, or Evasion?

One of the biggest phenomenon to hit the Christian Church in the last twenty years or so has been the Left Behind series of books by Tim LaHaye and Jerry B. Jenkins. These books were instant bestsellers, growing into a multi-volume series which even made the New York Times best sellers list.

Marketed as 'Christian fiction' these books are, nonetheless, predicated on events that

LaHaye and Jenkins believe are biblically prophesied and will occur during the time after the so-called Pre-Tribulation Rapture. Basically authors LaHaye and Jenkins have crafted a world in which their eschatology appears quite plausible, and even realistic within the context of their stories.

According to these books, those who are 'left behind' are non-Christians, and are thus ineligible to be taken up, or 'raptured' during the 'first phase' of Christ's return; leaving them to face the seven-year Tribulation period which is to follow. With the sudden consummation of this event, the main characters are left to seek an explanation for what has just happened; beginning a quest for the truth that leads them to faith in Jesus Christ. In the process they are forced to battle the Beast/Antichrist and his demonic system, which is set up by satanically-led people to control the Earth, until the 'second phase' of the Rapture occurs. This, according to the authors, is the 'Glorious Appearing' and physical return of Jesus, who overthrows this satanic system, thus ushering in the Millennial Kingdom.

Much has been made of this series by its promoters and propagators, many of whom have tried to use it as a vehicle for salvation. The success of this series has also lead to the writing of a kid's version, or sub-series, and some movies. The problem is that in their sincere zeal to win souls for the Lord they don't preach repentance and salvation as found in the Gospel. Instead they preach the Dispensational Rapture doctrine.

This phenomenon is nothing new nor is it as uncommon as one might be tempted to believe. A number of years ago a friend of the authors, a brother in Christ named Joe, was invited to a 'prophecy night' at a church in south Calgary featuring the Left Behind movie. Once he heard this, Joe knew what to expect, telling a friend that, instead of hearing a message about the need for people to repent of their sin and seek forgiveness in Christ to avoid God's eternal judgement, they were going to be encouraged to become Christians to avoid the Tribulation!

His friend tried to rebuke him for being so cynical and judgmental about an event to which he had never been to before. Unfortunately, however, Joe was one hundred percent correct; something his friend discovered to his chagrin afterwards.

Whatever happened to simply preaching the Gospel as Christ commanded us to in Matthew 28:18-21? Granted, not all who believe in the Pre-Trib Rapture preach this instead of the Gospel. We have some Dispensational brothers who continue to preach the great truths of salvation by grace alone, through faith alone, in Jesus Christ alone. Unfortunately, however, there are many that are more interested in preaching the Pre-Trib Rapture than (or in addition to) the Gospel in order to convert souls; a serious error which needs to be avoided.

Consider the commotion created when the first Left Behind movie was released into theaters in many cities in Canada and the United States. This film, based on the book series, was not pitched as simply popular entertainment but as a great opportunity for evangelism. Unfortunately the movie puts forward more 'rapture' than Gospel, creating the impression that Christians are simply those seeking to escape worldly tribulation rather than people who have made their peace with God through Jesus Christ.

This is a serious blunder for two reasons. First, we are never given any indication in the New Testament that this was the type of evangelical preaching the apostles were engaged in. When the Apostle Peter stood up on the day of Pentecost and the Spirit of God descended with power, he said " … Repent and be baptized every one of you in the name of Jesus Christ for the forgiveness of your sins, and you will receive the gift of the Holy Spirit ... And with many other words he bore witness and continued to exhort them, saying, Save yourselves from this crooked generation" (Acts 2:38, 40).

The key word here is repent, that is, to turn from your sins and trust in Jesus Christ, the only one able to save you from them. This account lines up perfectly with the Apostle Paul's sermon to the heathen on Mars hill when he told them that God " ... commands all people everywhere to repent, because he has fixed a day on which he will judge the world in righteousness by a man whom he has appointed; and of this he has given assurance to all by raising him from the dead" (Acts 17:30-31).

Notice that Paul is speaking about a specific day, not several days, nor several events or phases leading up to it. He says that it is an appointed day and, therefore, must be speaking about the final judgement where those who are judged will be thrown into the lake of fire (Revelation 20:11-15). His message was a warning to flee that day, not so they could avoid the Tribulation but to avoid eternal damnation.

In another instance, when Paul was imprisoned and under the care of the governor

Felix, he " ... reasoned (with him) of righteousness, self-control, and the coming judgement ... " (Acts 24:25). This judgement he was speaking of was not the seven-year period of Tribulation but the specifically appointed day of judgement which is to come for all those who die in their sins. Upon hearing this terrifying account " ... Felix was alarmed ... " (Acts 24:25), which is the exact effect the preaching of God's righteous law should have on an individual who has been convicted of their sin. Paul reasoned of righteousness, God's righteousness, not grace, nor love, but of the eternal justice of God's holy law against sin in order to prepare them for the message of God's grace and love.

That is not the message being preached today. By and large, at church, on TV, and through various books, publications, and the internet, people are being told that terrible events are going to come to pass upon the Earth and, if they want to avoid them they have to come to Christ so they will be raptured before it all comes to pass. But what they are not being told is that they need salvation because they may die at any moment and have to face God's justice and wrath because they will die in their sins.

The Bible says, " ... it is appointed for man to die once, and after that comes judgement" (Hebrews 9:27). It also says, "But thanks be to God, who gives us the victory through our Lord Jesus Christ" (1 Corinthians 15:57). The judgement the Apostle speaks of belongs to those who die in their sins apart from Christ, while the victory is solely to those who are in Christ. It doesn't belong to those who have been, or will be, 'caught up' in the hoped-for Pre-Trib Rapture, or to the so-called 'Tribulation Saints' who come to Jesus during that time of trouble. It belongs to all who have ever received the sacrifice of the Lord at Calvary since the time of the Apostles, and all the way back to the Old Testament saints who were saved by faith through the things which were ordained as a foreshadowing of Christ (Hebrews 11).

If people think otherwise, they are playing Russian roulette with their eternal souls. We need Christ for salvation, not to avoid the Tribulation. Period! Whether they die tomorrow, in the next 12 seconds, or at the hands of the demonic forces let loose on the world during the Tribulation, they need to be reassured of their eternal destiny not their temporal one; something many people may lose sight of in their hope of being 'raptured' before those dark times.

If you encounter unsaved people, your first duty is to warn them they could die tonight and be plunged into hell, *"where their worm does not die and the fire is not quenched"* (Mark 9:48). Don't tell them to flee to Christ to avoid persecution, via a Pre-Trib Rapture; warn them about the eternal wrath of God if they die in their sins! As Paul wrote: "Therefore, knowing the fear of the Lord, we persuade others ... " (2 Corinthians 5:11).

Secondly, this kind of evangelism has never been found in any portion of Church history, except in modern times. Probably the most glaring proof of this can be observed in the ministries of the men whom God used to spark the Great Awakening of the eighteenth century. George Whitefield was one of these men.

Whitefield was born in 1714 in the Bell Inn at Gloucester. In 1732 he attended Oxford University in London, England and became a member of a group called the Holy Club.

This organization was started by Charles Wesley and led by his brother John Wesley. The Holy Club was focused around the notion that they could perform good works in order to merit salvation, completely ignoring the biblical doctrine of justification by grace alone, through faith alone, in Christ alone. In 1735 Whitefield came to an understanding of this glorious truth, a truth he would expound continually and with great force and impact.

At the beginning of his open-air preaching ministry Whitefield went into a district adjacent to Bristol, England, called Kingswood. This was a large coal mining community with hundreds of miners and their families, where no church or school had ever been built for them, and where outsiders seldom ventured to go. Describing the impact on these people of his outdoor preaching, he said: "Having no righteousness of their own to renounce, they were glad to hear of a Jesus who was a friend of publicans and sinners, and came not to call the righteous but sinners to repentance. The first discovery of their being affected was to see the white gutters made by the tears which plentifully fell down their black cheeks, as they came out of their coal pits. Hundreds and hundreds of them were soon brought under deep convictions, which, as the event proved, happily ended in a sound and thorough conversion."[55]

---

[55] Arnold A. Dallimore, George Whitefield: God's Anointed Servant in the Great Revival of the Eighteenth Century, pg. 47, abridged version.

Such a testimony is only given by those who have been convicted of their sins and have found salvation in Jesus Christ. This is what Whitefield preached: that people need to repent of their sin and believe on the Lord Jesus Christ, who is able to save them.

When Whitefield ventured to the American Colonies he was requested to go to Northampton, MA, by the famed Jonathan Edwards. Edwards preached the well-known sermon, 'Sinners in the Hand of an Angry God,' and was a recognized leader of the Great Awakening in the colonies; he is often referred to as 'America's greatest mind.'

In his request to Whitefield, Edwards wrote " ... It has been with refreshment of soul that I have heard of one raised up in the Church of England to revive the mysterious, spiritual, despised, and exploded doctrines of the Gospel ... "[56] It was the doctrines of the Gospel which Whitefield revived and preached to sinners, and not those of the Pre-Trib Rapture.

In another instance a man at a service in Boston said that Whitefield, "After urging, 'Let not the fires of eternity be kindled against you!' pointing to a flash of lightning he [Whitefield]

---

[56] Ibid. pg. 88-89.

cried, 'See there! It is a glance from the angry eye of Jehovah! Hark!' ... "[57] In this Whitefield was following in the footsteps of the Puritans, and preached the same gospel they did, in almost the same place where they landed.

Dr. W G T Shedd, a 17th century Puritan minister, wrote in the preface to his book, 'Sermons To The Natural Man,' " ... If I have not preached redemption so fully as I have analyzed sin, it is because it is my deliberate conviction that just now the first and hardest work to be done by the preacher, for the natural man, is to produce in him some sensibility upon the subject of sin. Conscience needs to become consciousness ... "[58]

The Reformers preached an identical message, and all of them got it straight from the Scriptures. We must do likewise. Instead of telling men and women to be saved so that they may escape the Tribulation, we need to show them just how terrible their sin is before God so that they will flee to the Saviour. They need to know that they stand condemned by the Holy Law of God, and are under His wrath, before

---

[57] Ibid. pg. 91.

[58] W G T Shedd, Sermons to the Natural Man, pg. III.

they can be led to Christ who alone can save them (Acts 4:12).

If we fail to do this and preach, instead, the Pre-Trib Rapture, then we may cause many souls to be shipwrecked upon the rocks of damnation. We pray that this may not be the case.

5

The Blessed Hope and the Glorious Appearing: A Biblical Perspective

One of the most important things to understand about the differences between the Pre and Post-Tribulation Rapture doctrines are the definitions of the Blessed Hope and the Glorious Appearing as found in Titus 2:13 which says, "waiting for our blessed hope, the appearing of the glory of our great God and Savior Jesus Christ,"

To those who believe and propagate Pre-Trib Rapture teachings, the Blessed Hope *is* the Pre-Trib Rapture, while the Glorious Appearing is the event which takes place when Christ descends seven years after the Tribulation period to execute judgement on the earth. But is this really the case?

Tim LaHaye, referring to Titus 2:13, says, "Paul's 'Blessed Hope' is the Rapture, for it is unique to the Church. No one else will take part in it."[59] He then goes on to say, "The Glorious Appearing, on the other hand, is not for the Christian but for the remnant at the end of the Tribulation. It will primarily affect the Jews and those who have been good to them and who have somehow survived the Tribulation."[60] Unfortunately LaHaye does not give any Scripture for making such a claim. He provides no exegesis on Titus 2:13, and doesn't draw on any other parts of the Bible to try to prove his point.

---

[59] Tim LaHaye, The Rapture: Who Will Face the Tribulation? pg. 71.

[60] Ibid. pg. 71.

The reason for this is he can't! The Blessed Hope and the Glorious Appearing happen at the same time. They occur together and are inseparable one from the other.

When the Apostle Paul wrote Titus 2:13 he was not talking about two events separated by seven years, yet that is what LaHaye and the Dispensational crowd clings too. Taking deliberate license with English grammar, they claim that the word *and,* in this verse, is a separating term when, in reality, it's not.

Indeed, when you look at the verse it is clear that Paul does not separate the Blessed Hope from the Glorious Appearing, he connects them. This is obvious because he begins the verse with the idea that Christians are actually looking for both of these events to happen. There cannot, therefore, be any significant separation in time between these incidents. If there is, it would make the Glorious Appearing superfluous to those who have been raptured. It would also make it pointless for Paul to tell 'raptured' Believers to be looking since, as any Dispensationalist worth his salt would argue, they cannot predict the date of the Blessed Hope (the Rapture), or even the Glorious Appearing. They would already be with the Lord and have to witness it from above if they can.

The Dispensationalist, however, must believe that the Blessed Hope and the Glorious Appearing happen seven years apart; with the former representing the Pre-Trib Rapture of the Church, and the latter, the return of Christ after the Tribulation. The problem is that they have failed to understand exactly what the nature of the Rapture is, a charge they would furiously deny. They see the Rapture as partially a resurrection and partially a translation (i.e. the catching up of living Believers), thinking that the translation is not the same as the Resurrection, which is incorrect.

The Rev. Todd Baker, Th.M., a Staff Theologian at Zola Levitt Ministries, said in an e-mail to us that, " ... the Rapture not only involves a resurrection but a translation of those who are living that will never see death."[61] It is self-evident, in Rev. Baker's comments, that he believes the translation is somehow different from the Resurrection. This distinction is made simply because the Saints who are translated are alive at the time of Christ's return and, therefore, "will never see death" as was in the case of Enoch (Hebrews 11:5). It is also self-evident,

---

[61] Rev. Todd Baker, Th.M., a Staff Theologian at Zola Levitt Ministries, www.levitt.com.

from Rev. Baker's statement, that a resurrection can, therefore, only refer to the Believer who has already experienced a bodily death and was now going to experience a bodily restoration of life; although in a body raised incorruptible and spiritual (1 Corinthians 15:42-58).

When Paul, however, was defending the doctrine of the Resurrection to the Corinthian church he made no such distinction. He wrote that the Resurrection and the translation were going to happen *at once* because they were the **same event**. "Behold! I tell you a mystery. We shall not all sleep, but we shall all be changed, in a moment, in the twinkling of an eye, at the last trumpet. For the trumpet will sound, and the dead will be raised imperishable, and we shall be changed" (1 Corinthians 15:51-52).

The proper theological understanding of the Resurrection, therefore, is when the body, whether physically living or dead, sheds its corruption and mortality, and God imparts immortality to it by His sovereign will. It is not simply a *restoring* of life to the body, as the Dispensationalists claim, but the discarding of corruption and the putting on of incorruption. "For this perishable body must put on the imperishable, and this mortal body must put on immortality" (1 Corinthians 15:53).

Paul says virtually the same thing in 1 Thessalonians 4:16-17. But Rev. Baker, and other Dispensationalists, want you to believe that the Rapture involves two distinct events or actions; a bodily resurrection for the dead, and a translation for the living.

To them they are not one and the same thing, nor can they be. Why? For the simple reason that the Pre-Trib Rapture doctrine is built upon this; something we will explain further in chapter 7.

More significantly, though, LaHaye and the Dispensationalists believe that what makes the Blessed Hope truly blessed is because Christians will not be on earth during the time of Tribulation. He writes: "If Christ does not rapture His church before the Tribulation begins, much of the hope is destroyed, and thus it becomes a blasted hope rather than a blessed one."[62]

Is this the case? Is the Blessed Hope the Pre-Tribulation Rapture? George Eldon Ladd makes an astonishing observation in reference to that very claim. He says, "The Question of the relationship of the Rapture to that of the

---

[62] Tim LaHaye, The Rapture: Who Will Face the Tribulation? pg.71.

Tribulation may be set in proper perspective if we first survey the history of prophetic interpretation. The hope of the Church throughout the early centuries was the second coming of Christ, not a pretribulation rapture. If the Blessed Hope is in fact a Pretribulation rapture, then the Church has never known that hope through most of its history, for the idea of a pretribulation rapture did not appear in prophetic interpretation until the nineteenth century."[63]

Furthermore, in Scripture the word *"blessed,"* in this context, means "happy," and the word *"hope"* means "expectation." So what we are dealing with here is a "happy expectation." It is a Biblical doctrine that generates within us a deep-rooted happiness as we look forward in expectation for this event to come to pass.

Paul, in Romans 8:18-19, says, "For I consider that the sufferings of this present time are not worth comparing with the glory that is to be revealed to us. For the creation waits with eager longing for the revealing of the sons of God." He goes on to explain that all of Creation was subjected to corruption because of man's sin, and that when believers are gloriously raised

---

[63] George Eldon Ladd, The Blessed Hope, pg. 19.

creation shall also be delivered from this same bondage. "For the creation was subjected to futility, not willingly, but because of him who subjected it, in hope that the creation itself will be set free from its bondage to corruption and attain the freedom of the glory of the children of God. For we know that the whole creation has been groaning together in the pains of child birth until now. And not only the creation, but we ourselves, who have the first fruits of the Spirit, groan inwardly as we wait eagerly for adoption as sons, the redemption of our bodies." (Romans 8:20-23).

    Paul is saying that the groaning is a result of our waiting and longing for the redemption of the body (i.e. the Resurrection) that we may finally be rid of this sinful, corrupted flesh. This is the anticipation and desire of every true believer. He reaffirms this in Romans 7:24 when he says, "Wretched man that I am! Who will deliver me from this body of this death?" (Romans 7:24).

    In all of this we can rightly understand that the Blessed Hope is actually the Resurrection; the time in which we will be raised and glorified and furnished with a new body. The Apostle John puts it like this: "Beloved, we are God's children now, and what we will be has not yet appeared; but we know that when he appears we shall be like him, because we shall see him as he is" (1 John 3:2). We will have resurrection bodies and this sinful flesh will be finally done away with because " ... flesh and blood cannot inherit the kingdom of God, nor does the perishable inherit the imperishable" (1 Corinthians 15:50). This is the true hope and expectation of the Believer, and must not be overshadowed by some vain hope of avoiding the Tribulation!

The Apostle Paul affirms this. He says in Philippians 1:21, "For to me to live is Christ, and to die is gain." It is gain for the Believer when he dies because he will then dwell with the Lord where sin can no longer affect him, awaiting the Resurrection to live eternally without the devastating effect of the fall. What more Blessed Hope could there be than this? So when Paul says that we're "waiting for our Blessed Hope ..." (Titus 2:13) he is speaking expressly about the Resurrection and not about a two-phase return of Christ, with some Pre-Tribulation Rapture event that will take away Believers and leave the rest behind.

LaHaye's view, and the Dispensationalists, is not what the Scriptures plainly teach. Despite what they say, the Blessed

The First Resurrection: The Historic Hope of the Church

Hope is not the Pre-Trib Rapture; it is actually the Resurrection of the Saints to glory and eternal life.

In another place in his book LaHaye, speaking of the approaching Tribulation, says, "The purpose of these torturous days will be to provide humanity a seven year period in which to make their decision to accept Christ—or to accept Antichrist, the very embodiment of evil. It is a comfort to all Christians to know they do not have to face the coming storm of judgement. That is precisely why the Rapture is called 'the Blessed Hope.'"[64]

This is another one of LaHaye's extraordinary and unsupported claims. How does he know that this "seven year period" is to give those who are left behind a chance to "make their decision to accept Christ—or to accept Antichrist?" He is only assuming this to legitimize his claim that the Pre-Tribulation Rapture becomes the Blessed Hope because it leads to Christians being taken away before the Tribulation begins; never mind that those who become Christians during this horrific time must endure the wrath of the devil.

---

[64] Tim LaHaye, The Rapture: Who Will Face the Tribulation?, pg. 97-98.

For LaHaye and other Dispensationalists, these are the 'Johnny-come-lately's' of Christianity. They have missed the Pre-Trib Rapture bus and for that, presumably, they will suffer all the punishments that he believes God would never allow the Church to endure. That makes them, in effect, second-class Believers; and the cannon fodder of the Faith.

So while the rest of us are enjoying the benefits of being the bride in the bridal chamber for a seven-year honeymoon, our apparently luckless brethren on Earth suffer horribly the wrath of the Antichrist that we just happened to avoid. That is the real meaning (and problem) of the Dispensational "Blessed Hope" and why it is completely unbiblical. Yet this is what several ministers in effect are teaching to their congregations today.

The modern church, however, seems to have missed this point. Instead of teaching the Rapture *as* the First Resurrection, it has been made a doctrine in and of itself. Yet Paul, in 1 Thessalonians 4 and 1 Corinthians 15, is not talking about the Rapture, per se, but is really explaining the manner in which the Resurrection will take place. He is taking a known doctrine (the Resurrection) and breaking it down into exactly how it will happen. "In a moment, in the twinkling of an eye, at the last trump: for the trumpet shall sound, and the dead shall be raised incorruptible, and we shall be changed" (1 Corinthians 15:52), and, "For the Lord himself will descend from heaven with a cry of command, with the voice of the archangel, and with the sound of the trumpet of God. And the dead in Christ will rise first. Then we, who are alive, who are left, will be caught up together with them in the clouds, to meet the Lord in the air ... " (1 Thessalonians 4:16-17).

To teach others that the Pre-Trib Rapture is the Blessed Hope, rather than the Resurrection, is a huge misrepresentation of what the Scriptures really teach and should be left behind, pun intended. The other event, the Glorious Appearing, happens at the same time; they are, in fact, the same event, not unique events separated by any perceivable length of time.

The Glorious Appearing is where Christ is manifest to the entire world when he returns. Paul says in 2 Thessalonians, " ... the Lord Jesus is revealed from heaven with his mighty angels in flaming fire, inflicting vengeance on those who do not know not God and on those who do not obey the gospel of our Lord Jesus" (2 Thessalonians 1:7-8). This is precisely why it is titled the Glorious Appearing, because Christ will return gloriously.

The writer of Hebrews said that the Lord will, " … appear a second time, not to deal with sin but to save those who are eagerly waiting for him" (Hebrews 9:28). This means Jesus will be completely apart from any sin, and will resurrect the Saints in glory.

The Bible teaches that Christ took on the form of sinful flesh (Romans 8:3), although He is without sin Himself (2 Corinthians 5:21). But when He returns, having banished sin in the flesh by His own sacrifice, He will be in the form of His glorious resurrection body. Paul affirms this in 1 Corinthians 15:50 saying, "I tell you this, brothers: flesh and blood cannot inherit the kingdom of God, nor does the perishable inherit the imperishable."

Our flesh and blood is corrupted by sin. But, as Christians we have been freed from sin through Christ's sacrifice. Being, therefore, translated into His Kingdom ("For this perishable body must put on the imperishable, and this mortal body must put on immortality …" (1 Corinthians 15:53)) we can say, as Paul said, " … then shall come to pass the saying that is written: 'Death is swallowed up in victory'" (1 Corinthians 15:54). Jesus described this event in more detail. He said in Matthew 24:30, regarding His second coming, "Then will appear in heaven the sign of the Son of Man, and then all the tribes of the earth will mourn, and they will see the Son of Man coming on the clouds of heaven with power and great glory." Again, we see that His return is not in humility and weakness, as was His first coming, but in power and great glory.

In the book of the Revelation, John expounds this event even further. He writes, "Then I saw heaven opened, and behold, a white horse! The one sitting on it is called Faithful and True, and in righteousness he judges and makes war. His eyes are like a flame of fire, and on his head are many diadems, and he has a name written that no one knows but he himself. He is clothed in a robe dipped in blood, and the name by which he is called is The Word of God" (Revelation 19:11-13). The rider, the Faithful and True, is none other than Jesus Christ, for John uses the name, the Word of God, just as he did in the Gospel which he wrote (see John 1:1-5). John also says the rider's robe is dipped in blood, which represents the judgement of his enemies as he is the one who treads the winepress of the wrath of God: "Then I looked, and behold, a white cloud, and seated on the cloud one like a son of man, with a golden crown on his head, and a sharp sickle in his hand ... So the angel swung his sickle across the earth and gathered the grape harvest of the earth and threw it into the great winepress of the wrath of God. And the winepress was trodden outside the city, and blood flowed from the winepress, as high as the horse bridle ..." (Revelation 14:14, 19-20).

Acts 1:9-11 says, "And when he [Jesus] had said these things, as they were looking on, he was lifted up, and a cloud took him out of their sight. And while they were gazing into heaven as he went, behold, two men stood by them in white robes, and said, 'Men of Galilee, why do you stand looking into heaven? This Jesus, who was taken up from you into heaven, will come in the same way as you saw him go into heaven." This verse tells us specifically that Jesus will return to the Earth, and will do so in "*the same way.*" Although Luke, the author of Acts, does not mention any of the details revealed to John in his prophesies later on, the event will occur in the same manner He left; visibly, from through the clouds, and landing physically on the earth. He never said Christ will come back partially, resurrect Believers, leave again, and then return in the Glorious Appearing for a supposed 'second phase' of His return as LaHaye and the Dispensationalists assert.

Christ is indeed coming back the way Scripture teaches. If the supposed Pre-Trib Rapture took place, however, no one would see Him because Dispensationalists believe that this event will be sudden and unseen. Christians would just disappear and meet Him in the air, en-route to the "bridal chamber" for seven years. If Christ comes back to Earth in the Dispensational Glorious Appearing, the Believers would be with him, and, therefore, unable to watch His return as He descends from Heaven, as Luke said they would.

By putting all of these verses together we can clearly see the sequence of events that will take place. Christ is coming back in power, and great glory. He will return from Heaven through the clouds and land physically on the Earth. As all of this is taking place we will witness His coming. At that moment, in the *"twinkling of an eye"* as Paul said, we will be translated (resurrected) to glory and return with Him. As stated above, these events are unique but they indeed happen at the same time.

All of this glorious prophetic truth will be dealt with in greater detail in later chapters as we continue to put all of the pieces together concerning the Resurrection. It is our earnest prayer that you, the readers, continue to search the Word diligently for yourselves to see if these things are so.

6

Signs of the Times: A Biblical Understanding of Christ's Imminent Return

One of the pillars of the Pre-trib Rapture view is the idea of Immanency. This is the thought that the Lord Jesus Christ could return and rapture His Church at any moment, without any signs or events to precede it.

LaHaye espouses the idea that you cannot underestimate the importance of Immanency in the life of a Christian. He says, "Historically, belief in the any-moment coming of Christ has three vital effects on Christians and their churches. 1. It produces holy living in an unholy society ... 2. It produces an evangelistic church of soul-winning Christians. When we believe Christ could appear at any moment, we seek to share Him with our friends lest they be left behind at His coming ... 3. Belief in the imminent return of Christ impels Christians and churches to develop a worldwide missionary vision of reaching the lost for Christ ... Believing in the soon coming of Christ for his church will have a profound effect on the way we live. It's much easier to 'set your affections on things above, not on the things of this earth' (Colossians 3:2) if we believe that Christ could come at any moment."[65]

Herb Hirt, another Dispensational thinker, supports LayHaye's view. In the article, 'Perhaps Today' (the Friends of Israel Gospel Ministry magazine, 'Israel my Glory') he wrote, "... immanency is important for the spiritual health of every believer and the church as a whole ... Ultimately, the doctrine of immanency is not a question of eschatology as much as it is a

---

[65] Ibid. pg. 21-22.

question of obedience and faith. Will we, as believers, live our lives in a way that prepares us to meet the Lord at any moment?"[66]

Reasoning such as this sounds plausible at first glance but is it really Scriptural? The shocking truth is that it is not. The implications of these statements are also very dangerous.

In a nutshell, LaHaye believes that if you do not believe in a sudden, unexpected Rapture, you are not impelled to live a holy life (be sanctified), preach the Gospel, or support others to be preachers of the Gospel! In effect, LaHaye is saying that those who do not believe in the at-any-moment, secret rapture, are men and women who care not for the souls of others.

The Bible, however, refutes both these men. Colossians 3:2-5 and 8-10 commands all Christians (irrespective of the claims made by LaHaye and Hirt), to "Set your minds on things that are above, not on things that are on the earth. For you have died, and your life is hidden with Christ in God. When Christ who is your life appears, then you also will appear with him in glory. Put to death therefore what is earthly in you: sexual immorality, impurity, passion, evil desire, and covetousness, which is idolatry ...

---

[66] Herb Hirt, Israel My Glory, Perhaps Today, pg.15.

But now you must put them all away: anger, wrath, malice, slander, and obscene talk from your mouth. Do not lie to one another, seeing that you have put off the old self with its practices and have put on the new self, which is being renewed in knowledge after the image of its creator."

As Believers, we accept, without reservation, that we should continue to live holy lives and preach the Gospel, praying that those efforts would be used of God to save souls for His Kingdom. By the same token, however, we adamantly oppose the Pre-Trib/Dispensationalist notion that Christ's supposed sudden, at-any-moment return should be the prime motivation behind it. Even in the verse quoted above, we readily observe that Paul informs us that we have already put off the "old man" and have put on the new. The exhortation, therefore, is given so that we may manifest outwardly the change which has already taken place inwardly.

Furthermore, God has specifically told us to be holy, not because of a sudden, any-moment rapture, but because He is Holy. 1 Peter 1:15-16 says, "but as he who called you is holy, you also be holy in all your conduct, since it is written, 'You shall be holy, for I am holy.'"

The truth of the matter is that sanctification is two-fold. It happens first at salvation, setting the Believer apart from the rest of the world in the eyes of God. 1 Corinthians 6:11 says, " ... But you were washed, you were sanctified, you were justified in the name of the Lord Jesus Christ and by the Spirit of our God." Acts 20:32 says, "And now I commend you to God and to the word of his grace, which is able to build you up and to give you the inheritance among all those who are sanctified."

First off, Believers are already sanctified, or "set apart," for the Master's use. Secondly, the Bible says that God has planned for those who are His to eventually bear the image of His Son. This can be understood as the practical working of sanctification, whereby God continually works in us so that we may be " ... conformed to the image of his Son ... " (Romans 8:29).

The seed of our holiness was sown in our lives at salvation and will bear fruit if we are truly saved (John 15:1-8). This fruit is the best sign of our sanctification, not some secret event that is supposed to occur without any preceding evidence.

So when those who preach the Pre-Trib Rapture make the claim that this doctrine is important because it *"prepares us"* (Believers) to live a holy life" in the midst of an unholy world, they ignore the rest of the Scriptures which teach that our holiness is predicated upon our salvation, and the work God does in us in order to bring us to maturity (Philippians 1:6).

In regard to LaHaye's second point, that only the Pre-Trib Rapture doctrine "produces an evangelistic Church of soul-winning Christians" because they don't want their friends to be "left behind at His coming," he has completely misunderstood the purpose of preaching. Jesus said, " … All authority in heaven and on earth has been given to me. Go therefore and make disciples of all nations, baptizing them in the name of the Father and of the Son and of the Holy Spirit, teaching them to observe all that I have commanded you. And behold, I am with you always, to the end of the age." (Matthew 28:18-20). He never said, "Do this because I'm coming at an hour you don't expect, and if you're not ready when I do show up, I won't rapture you. Then you'll have to endure seven years of tribulation while the rest of us party it up in Heaven."

When we preach the Gospel, our motivation comes from a love for our Lord, a desire to obey God (who gave us salvation, and all spiritual blessings in Heaven), and a love for lost souls. It is not driven by a fear of missing the secret rapture. Thus the claim that only a belief in the Pre-Trib Rapture is necessary to our sanctification, and as a motivator to preach the Gospel, is ridiculous.

For the non-Dispensationalist, the imminent return of Jesus Christ is understood differently than for the Dispensationalist. As we mentioned earlier, the latter believes that, in order for this event to be considered 'imminent,' there can and will be no prophetic signs preceding it. Dwight Pentecost says, "Many signs were given to the nation Israel, which would precede the Second Advent, so that the nation might be living in expectancy when the time of His coming should draw nigh. Although Israel could not know the day nor the hour when the Lord will come, yet they can know that their redemption draweth nigh through the fulfillment of these signs. To the church no such signs were ever given." [67]

This assertion is blatantly false. The Lord Jesus commands us in the gospels to watch for the signs of His return. Mark 13:29 clearly says that " … when you see these things taking place,

---

[67] J. Dwight Pentecost, Things To Come: A Study In Biblical Eschatology, pg 202-203.

you know that he is near, at the very gates." How can we 'know' unless we are aware. And how can we be aware unless we watch? Why, in fact, would the Lord show us signs of His coming if we are not to 'watch' out for them?

This makes no sense. But that doesn't stop the Dispensationalists. They claim that this 'watching' is really for the Lord and not for the signs which lead up to Him. Dwight Pentecost says, "Such passages as 1 Thessalonians 5:6; Titus 2:13; Revelation 3:3 all warn the believer to be watching for the Lord Himself, not for signs that would precede His coming."[68]

Unfortunately Pentecost does not even hint at the context of the passages he is referring to, which are actually inundated with prophetic signs that are to come. In Matthew 24:33 Christ says, "So also, when you see all these things, you know that he is near, at the very gates."

The Dispensationalists' response to this is that Christ is speaking specifically to the Jews during the time of the Tribulation, and that this verse is not relevant for non-Jews. But a conclusion like this can only be borne out of the belief that the Pre-Trib Rapture has already occurred and, therefore, Christ cannot be

---

[68] Ibid., pg. 203

speaking about the Church. This is strange given that, at the beginning of the chapter, it was the disciples who came to Him and asked, "when will these things be, and what will be the sign of your coming, and of the close of the age?" (Matthew 24:3).

Mark 13:24-37, start to finish, Jesus is telling His Disciples about the end times and that they should watch for the signs of His coming that they might prepare for it. He is not talking to the un-raptured 'Church,' 'Tribulation Saints,' or to unbelieving people, but to His disciples; in other words, those that follow Him.

He says, plainly, "From the fig tree learn its lesson: as soon as its branch becomes tender and puts out its leaves, you know that summer is near. So also, when you see these things taking place, know that he is near, at the very gates" (Mark 13:28-30). If we cannot understand these verses for what they say, then what about the Dispensationalists who claim to be the champions of a literal interpretation of the Scriptures? This claim will be discussed further in the next chapter and its errors will be exposed.

In a further attempt to substantiate his views, however, Dr. Pentecost also quotes what Chafer has to say in reference to what the

Reformers believed concerning Immanency. He says, "Luther wrote, 'I believe that all the signs which are to precede the last days have already appeared. Let us not think that the Coming of Christ is far off; let us look up with heads lifted up; let us expect our Redeemer's coming with longing and cheerful mind, … Calvin also declares … 'Scripture uniformly enjoins us to look with expectation for the advent of Christ.'"[69] This is very interesting in light of the fact that the Reformers were Amillennial in their eschatological outlook and not Premillennial as both Post and Pre-Tribbers are (Pentecost simply says the Reformers held a 'different view,' but does not explain what that view is).

Luther, one of the greatest known Reformers, claimed that all of the signs have already passed, while the Dispensationalists believe there are no signs to be had. Regarding John Calvin, another great Reformer, Pentecost even goes so far to assert that he was indeed a supporter of the Pre-Trib Rapture (in fact Calvin only mentioned the advent, which is in reference to the physical appearing of Christ with power and great glory).

---

[69] Ibid., pg. 203-204

The truth is that the Reformers did, in fact, believe in Immanency, but it is not the same view of Immanency held by the Dispensationalists. They believed in the preceding signs of Christ's return, but they NEVER held to a Pre-Trib Rapture or any premillennial position at all! Despite this, many Dispensationalists, in seeking to legitimize their view as being consistent with Church doctrine and history, love to quote them and talk as if they are walking in their footsteps.

The real crux of the division between the Dispensationalist and the Reformers of old, however, was the latter's motivation to save people from the clutches of Roman Catholicism and to know Christ personally. They did not do this because they felt His return was imminent and secret, and that people needed to become Believers so that they can be raptured. They did this because they wanted to save souls from eternal damnation.

Luther, Calvin, and the rest knew that the wrath of God abides on those who do not believe (John 3:36), and they, like the Apostle Paul, knowing the fear of the Lord, persuaded people to be saved (2 Corinthians 5:11). Thus to say that a Pre-Trib Rapture view is necessary, or even required, to bring people to salvation, is a slap in the face to the very people Dispensationalists (falsely) claim to be their inspiration and supporters of their position.

Here is an illustration which might be able to help us understand a proper way of viewing Immanency. A pregnant woman knows that there is approximately nine months after conception when her baby will be born. As she begins to progress in her pregnancy she becomes keenly aware of the signs of her impending labor. Then, suddenly, despite all the signs, contractions come upon her, unexpectedly. In the process, her water may break, which is an even more telling sign that the baby's birth is imminent. Yet, in all this, the woman still does not know the day or the hour when these events will take place; all she has are the signs and the foreknowledge of them until, finally, the infant begins to crown and birth is inevitable.

This is what the Apostle Paul conveys when he talks about the last days in 2 Thessalonians. Like a good doctor he mentions the signs of the times, knowing the order of the events that will take place before the consummation of the age, but without saying he knows the exact day or hour. "Now concerning the coming of our Lord Jesus Christ and our being gathered together to him, we ask you, brothers, not to be quickly shaken in mind or alarmed, either by a spirit or a spoken word, or a letter seeming to be from us, to the effect that the day of the Lord has come. Let no one deceive you in any way. For that day will not come, unless the rebellion comes first, and the man of lawlessness is revealed, the son of destruction" (2 Thessalonians 2:1-3).

The Thessalonians of that time were apparently troubled by an erroneous letter. Some false prophets or teachers had ingratiated themselves into their group and were, apparently, stirring up this young church to believe that the day of Christ (His second advent) was at hand. But Paul did his best to quickly squash this false notion by pointing out that two key events must take place before Jesus returns: a falling away, and the revealing of the man of sin (the Antichrist). Yet, these days, large numbers of Christians are convinced of a "secret snatching away" before the Tribulation, without any signs.

How does this line up with the admonition of Paul to the Thessalonians, who he specifically told to watch for these two events? Is it possible to watch for something that you will never be able to see? This is but one of the many contradictions that results from a Dispensational interpretation of Scripture. It's also interesting to note that Paul told the Thessalonians that he knew for a fact that the day of Christ was *not* yet at hand. This is diametrically opposite to the modern teaching on the second coming for Christ.

What we need is a proper biblical perspective and not some tainted understanding of events. As Christians, we accept that death is imminent for everyone and that if people do not believe in Christ for the forgiveness of their sins they will be eternally condemned by God. If, therefore, there is a doctrine of imminence let it be this one and not the confused reasoning of a secret Pre-Trib Rapture of the Church so they can evade the Tribulation.

We know that to be scriptural we must watch for the prevailing signs and seasons, not in order to identify the specific day or hour, but so that we may always be looking forward to our Lord's return in great power and glory. The signs and seasons, themselves representing a guide by which we can tell that our bodily redemption is near, should give us hope and comfort in both times of joy and in the worst tribulation that we may have to endure. As our Lord Jesus Christ said, most emphatically, "So also, when you see these things taking place, you know that he is near, at the very gates" (Mark 13:29; see also Mark 13:24-28).

7

The Proclaimed Monopoly: Dispensationalism and Literal Interpretation

The most interesting claim from the Dispensationalist camp is that they somehow have a monopoly on the literal method of interpreting the Scriptures. This claim has far-reaching implications to those who do not accept the validity of Dispensational theology and the Pre-Tribulation Rapture view.

In the modern Church, being a literal exegete is synonymous with someone who has orthodox or fundamental beliefs. Those who reject Dispensationalism (and hence a literal interpretation of the Scriptures) are seen as being akin to liberals or, in some cases, outright heretics. So, in the attempt to make sure no one defects from Dispensationalism, they try to paint every contrary view as less literal than their own, thus making themselves out to be the 'champions of Biblical truth.'

LaHaye, not surprisingly, supports this view. He says "The church (and, some believe, Old Testament saints) will be resurrected or raptured prior to that Tribulation ... After the seven year Tribulation Christ will come in His glorious appearing, destroy Antichrist and the False Prophet, and chain Satan in the bottomless pit. He will then set up His kingdom and rule the world with His saints ... This view is held by most fundamentalists and many evangelicals who take prophetic scriptures literally. As a general rule, the more a person accepts the Bible literally, the more likely he is to hold the pre-Tribulation view."[70]

---

[70] Tim LaHaye, The Rapture: Who Will Face the Tribulation?, pg. 104-107.

LaHaye reinforces this later on, saying, "… As a general rule, those who take prophecy as literally as they take other scriptures are prone to hold to the Pre-Trib view."[71] He then quotes Dr. John Walvoord as an authority to add weight to his argument: " … Posttribulationism is the ordinary view of practically all amillenarians and postmillenarians. It is embraced by Roman Catholic and Greek Catholic; it is followed by many Protestant conservatives as well as modern liberals … "[72] This is a very clever device. By lumping Post-Trib, Amillennial, and Postmillennial Believers with heretics, and by not explaining the differences between those groups, LaHaye and Walvoord hope to undercut the credibility of these alternative views. In so doing they can then reaffirm the Dispensationalist claim to be the sole guardians of the truth.

As clever a device as this is, however, it comes across, at times, like a child's schoolyard ploy. By painting themselves as being the 'in crowd' they hope to draw people to their side, thereby isolating and diminishing those who

---

[71] Ibid. pg. 122.

[72] Ibid.

hold views contrary to their own. The fact that it may not be based on sound doctrine and biblical truth is immaterial; as long as their side appears to be popular with most Christians at large, they are winning the debate and hence have the right to set the standard upon which to judge all other views.

Dr. Dwight Pentecost makes the same claims as all the other supposed 'champions' of the literal method do. He says, "Pretribulation rapturism rests essentially on one major premise — the literal method of interpretation of the Scriptures. As a necessary adjunct to this, the pretribulationist believes in a dispensational interpretation of the Word of God ... "[73]

Notice Pentecost's subtle caveat to his claims of literalism. For him, like others in his camp, the Word of God is interpreted literally but in the context of a Pre-Trib view, and filtered through a Dispensational interpretation. But how can something be truly literal and, at the same time, require interpretation? It can't. But, like all Dispensationalists, Pentecost can't see through his own Pre-Trib haze to realize the inherent contradiction in his logic.

---

[73] J. Dwight Pentecost, Things To Come: A Study in Biblical Eschatology, pg. 193.

You can see this in the writings of others as well. In the August/September 2000 edition of the Friends of Israel Gospel Ministry magazine, "Israel My Glory," author David M. Levy says, "Those who hold the pretribulational view do so for the following reasons. First, they believe that the Scripture passages dealing with the Rapture must be interpreted literally, not allegorically ..."[74]

Gerald B. Stanton, in his book, 'Kept from the Hour: Biblical Evidence for the Pretribulational Return of Christ,' says, "It will be demonstrated that the sine qua non, the one thing indispensable to the premillennial view point — indeed, to orthodoxy itself — is that the Scriptures of God be understood in a normal, grammatical, literal fashion."[75] What is interesting about this is that Stanton not only states just what constitutes a "normal, grammatical, literal fashion" interpretation of the Scriptures but also admits that there are,

---

[74] David M. Levy, Israel My Glory, The Rapture Question, pg. 11. (Again, he means "literal" in the context of Dispensational thinking, not simply reading it and gaining the sense of it in the Biblical context.)

[75] Gerald B. Stanton, Kept From the Hour: Biblical Evidence for the Pretribulational Return of Christ, pg. 140.

indeed, other views of the timing of the Rapture among the Premillennialist camp. He writes, "There are four major positions among premillennialists as to the time of the rapture of the church ... pretribulational... partial rapture ... midtribulational ... posttribulational ... "[76] But just when you think he has opened the door to allowing even the possibility that a non-Dispensational view can also be derived literally, he falls back onto the now-typical cry that literalism belongs solely to those Premillennialists who are also Pre-Trib.

"It will then be demonstrated that both the midtribulationalists and the posttribulationalists violate this principle (that of the literal method of interpretation) whenever their systems demand it, thus throwing open the door to a spiritualizing or allegorizing method which has fostered modernism and which violates a consistent premillennial theology ..."[77] Stanton says.

Though Stanton is right in claiming that the literal method should be championed, his claims that the Post-Trib position needs to

---

[76] Ibid. pg. 17.

[77] Ibid., pg. 140

spiritualize whenever the system demands it are blatantly wrong and demonstrates just how desperate Dispensationalists are to cling to their self-appointed status as guardians of the truth. As you will see later on, it is the Pre-Tribbers themselves who twist Scripture to fit their system, while the Post-Trib, non-Dispensational position, is actually the most literal and biblically accurate.

Stanton's proof that Post Tribbers spiritualize comes from the fact that some have stated that the Tribulation period is not as severe as indicated in the Scriptures. He says, "Although post-tribulationalists do not completely spiritualize the Tribulation, it is not difficult to detect a strong inclination in that direction … They minimize its severity and try to tone down its judgements to the point that the Tribulation is no longer a unique period of unprecedented wrath, but merely another period of persecution upon the people of God and that no more severe than previous times of suffering … "[78] To that end, he quotes Norman S. McPherson, author of 'Triumph Through Tribulation,' who wrote, "Surely the church has been permitted to pass through many other

---

[78] Ibid. pg. 159.

periods of suffering and anguish so acute that if those who went through them should have to go through the Tribulation, they would not feel they had missed anything during their first period of trial."[79]

The problem is that Stanton is trying to paint every Post-Tribber with the same brush. As there are differences among Dispensationalists, there are also differences among non-Dispensationalists. For our part, we hold the view that the Tribulation is and will be a time of great and unparalleled suffering, the likes of which the world has not seen since the beginning of time (Matt. 24:21). Anyone who suggests otherwise is being unscriptural and wrong, whether he is Pre or Post Trib in his eschatology.

Where we depart from Stanton and the people in his camp, however, is that we see no contradiction in " ... having the church both purged and protected at the same time ... "[80] We are purged by the fires which are unleashed upon us by the Antichrist, yet we are protected and kept from God's wrath, which is poured out

---

[79] Ibid.

[80] Ibid. pg. 160.

upon wicked man. But this thought has never entered the minds of LaHaye (and others) who say, " … the hope and comfort aspect of the Rapture demands that we escape the Tribulation, being raptured out of this world before God's wrath is poured out."[81]

As for the glibly used accusation of spiritualization one need look no further than Dr. Pentecost. Pentecost says that one of his proofs for the Pre-Trib Rapture is Typology, which he defines as argument from analogy. He says, " … Scripture abounds in types which teach that those who walked by faith were delivered from the visitations of judgement which overtook the unbelieving. Such types are seen in the experience of Noah and Rahab, but perhaps the clearest illustration is that of Lot … If the presence of one righteous man prevented the outpouring of deserved judgement on the city of Sodom, how much more the presence of the church on earth will prevent the outpouring of divine wrath until after her removal."[82]

---

[81] Tim LaHaye, The Rapture: Who Will Face the Tribulation?, pg. 70.

[82] J. Dwight Pentecost, Things to Come: A Study in Biblical Eschatology, pg. 217-218

It would take an extreme leap of logic to show any learned person how the story of Sodom and Gomorrah can prove the Pre-Trib Rapture. It also underlines the fact that Dispensationalists like Pentecost do not consider those who might be saved during the Tribulation to be a part of the same Church or body of Believers as those who were 'Raptured' out before this period began, a point to which we will return to later.

Admittedly, Pentecost says that he is using this as an example of typology and one must presume that, in the context of this analogy, Lot and his family represent the Church, while the doomed cities represent the world. But if that is the case, one must also remember that Lot's wife turned back to the world and became a pillar of salt, while not only the people of Sodom and Gomorrah were destroyed but their entire city as well. Does Pentecost mean, therefore, that the world will also be destroyed after the Rapture, and that, while being raptured some Christians will also turn back upon the world and be condemned?

The problem is that he, like other Dispensationalists, glean only those things from the Bible that supports their views while dismissing those things that don't. Although

Pentecost says he is only using this as an analogy in order to " ... teach that those who walked by faith were delivered from the visitations of judgement which overtook the unbelieving" he only uses what he finds useful. The problem he has, however, is that he uses the story of Sodom and Gomorrah in error.

According to Peter, God turned " ... the cities of Sodom and Gomorrah to ashes (and) he condemned them to extinction, making them an example of what is going to happen to the ungoldy" (2 Peter 2:6). He didn't do it to show or prefigure the rapture but to show his wrath against sin while saving those that cling to him. As it is written " ... the Lord knows how to rescue the godly from trials, and to keep the unrighteous under punishment until the day of judgement" (2 Peter 2:9).

Clearly, Pentecost is grasping at straws. To those steeped in Dispensationalism, the Pre-Trib version is valid, even though it completely misses the fact that, unlike Sodom and Gomorrah (which were completely vaporized), there will be righteous people on the earth; the so-called 'Tribulation Saints' that LaHaye, Pentecost, and others are so enamored with.

Are these people, saved during the Tribulation, not to be considered as covered with the same righteousness as those who were raptured beforehand? Are they not part of the Church?

Dispensationalists often bring forth the claim that God will not unleash judgement upon the Earth while the Church is there. But are not those saved in the Tribulation part of the same Church or Body of Christ? Who are they then and what is their divine or spiritual standing?

This is a big problem for Dispensationalists to solve. If they claim that these Tribulation Saints are not part of the Church then they are saying Christ's body is divided; that the blood atonement of Jesus is one thing for those who are raised and raptured *before* the Tribulation and another for those saved *in* the Tribulation (a situation that further puts the lie to their supposed notion of having a monopoly on any literal interpretation of Scripture). This double-minded reasoning is quite contradictory, and not helpful to a clear understanding of the sense of Scripture.

To sum up: on the one hand Dispensationalists say that there has to be a Pre-Trib Rapture because God would not allow His Bride to go through this time of trial. And on the other hand they claim that the Jews, whom they believe are God's chosen people, along with the future Tribulation Saints (who are people of all nations saved during the Tribulation) will go through this time of trial.

The implications of this view are astounding if one considers it carefully. In effect Dispensationalists are saying there is something special about those who get raptured out before Tribulation, that the atonement for the and their salvation is somehow more special than those who are saved during this horrible period. Or does it really come down to what we said earlier about future Believers simply having missed the 'Pre-Trib Rapture bus' and must now suffer because they were deemed less worthy of avoiding the Tribulation as those who came to salvation before it started?

Is this the God the Dispensationalists are actually offering to those who follow their views? Is God, to them, a capricious being who seems to love less those who come to Christ after the Pre-Trib bus leaves the station, leaving them to suffer unimaginable horrors while the rest enjoy a party in Heaven? Really?

If the Dispensationalists want to play that game, that's fine. But then what of the story of Noah? In this typology you can see Christ (represented by the Ark), with the Church (represented by Noah and his family) in the midst of the Tribulation but shielded from God's judgement. Notice, however, that Noah and his family were not taken out of the world while terrible events took place around them. Rather they were guided safely through them until God's wrath upon the wicked was completed!

In reality Noah rightfully represents those redeemed by Christ who were saved by the ark of His body (that is, by His death), from the eternal wrath of God (1 Peter 3:20-21). Yet that doesn't stop Dispensationalists from claiming that it is the Post-Tribber who needs to 'spiritualize' to make his point while they see themselves as champions of the literal method. If they were truly being honest, however, they would admit that they themselves use analogies as much as anyone else and, quite often, more so since their eschatology habitually demands that they divide Scripture between those passages they claim are exclusively for and about the Church and those for and exclusively about Israel and the Jewish people.

A case in point is their position on the First Resurrection found in Revelation 20:5. According to this verse " … The rest of the dead did not come to life until the thousand years were ended. This is the first resurrection." If one reads the Book of Revelation it is evident that

Jesus' return takes place in Chapter 19, while the First Resurrection takes place in Chapter 20, *after* or at the end of the Tribulation. Now if the Rapture involves the Resurrection of the bodies of the dead Believers (along with the raising of the living to glorified bodies), and the First Resurrection takes place *after* the Tribulation, how do the Dispensationalists validate their view that there is such a thing as a Pre-Tribulation Rapture *and* maintain their claim of being biblically literal?

According to Todd Baker, "Revelation 20:4-5 must be understood within the proper context of the first resurrection. The first resurrection did not begin and end with the event recorded in Revelation 20:5. The first resurrection began with the resurrection of the Lord Jesus Christ who was the first fruits (1 Corinthians 15:22-23). The second phase of the first resurrection will occur at the Rapture of the Church. This will occur when the dead in Christ rise first and we who are alive shall be caught up with them to meet the Lord in the air (1 Thessalonians 4:14-18). Notice that the Rapture not only involves a resurrection but a translation of those who are living that will never see death. There is no such detail like this mentioned in Revelation 20:5. Only a resurrection is mentioned in that verse, no translation. So Revelation is not talking about the Rapture but rather the third stage that will complete the first resurrection (the two other phases being the resurrection of Christ some 2,000 years ago and the second phase being the Rapture of the Church sometime before the Tribulation begins). The part that will complete the first resurrection is the resurrection of the Tribulation Saints as clearly indicated in verse 4."[83]

Does this really sound literal? Does this sound like the understanding of Revelation 20:5 has arisen from a plain reading of the text? (Please note, we will discuss this verse in greater detail in the following chapter.)

Typology and analogy are important and should be understood clearly. That said, Bible scholars also should be able to discern, correctly, what genuinely supports their views, and what does not. Simply stretching portions of Scripture to meet your theological imperative is deceitful and quite dangerous, spiritually.

Clearly the oft-repeated charge that Post-Tribbers spiritualize while Pre-Tribbers are literal is unfounded, unprincipled and, quite patently,

---

[83] Rev. Todd Baker, ThM, a Staff Theologian at Zola Levitt Ministries, www.levit.com.

wrong. In truth, we sincerely believe that a person comparing both these positions will be able to judge for themselves who is literal and who is not.

Furthermore, just because some people have made a career out of taking liberties with the Scriptures does not mean that all people do. Nor does it mean that there are not points of agreement between Dispensationalists and non-Dispensationalists, or that fellowship should be denied or broken between members of these groups. Yet, by the same token, it is a grievous error (and potentially very divisive to the body of Christ) when those of the former try to lump those of the latter together with liberals and modernists due to the biblical stance they have taken.

This is the same tactic frequently used in politics, whereby one party defames the other by using words like 'scary,' 'uniformed,' or 'dangerous.' While this may be an expected and even effective tactic during a political campaign, it has no place among those seeking to discern what the Bible actually says.

The same is true here. Despite what LaHaye, Pentecost, Stanton, and others like to believe, they do not hold a monopoly on the literal method of interpretation. As we have already seen, and will again in the following chapters, their views not only lack the mantel literalism they are desperate to clothe themselves in, but are quite flawed when set against biblical evidence and the actual traditional view of the Church—Historic Premillennialism.

The Bible expressly commands us to "Do your best to present yourself to God as one approved, a worker who has no need to be ashamed, rightly handling the word of truth" (2 Timothy 2:15). As we continue to explore and validate, by Scripture, the position we have taken, we pray that you, our brothers and sisters, would likewise search the Scriptures and see if our claims are warranted. Correct us if you feel we are wrong, support us if you feel we are right. And may God receive all the Glory through our Lord Jesus Christ.

8

The *First* Resurrection on The *Last* Day

LaHaye says, "One objection to the pre-Tribulation rapture is that no one passage of Scripture teaches the two phases of Christ's coming separated by the Tribulation. This is true. But then, no one passage teaches a post-Tribulation or mid-Tribulation rapture, either. (And no passage teaches against the pre-Trib view.)"[84] That notion is flatly wrong. The

---

[84] Tim LaHaye, The Rapture: Who Will Face the Tribulation?, pg. 77.

Scriptures are very clear on the timing of the Resurrection (or Rapture), although not the precise day or hour, as Jesus said in Matthew 24:36: "But concerning that day and hour no one knows, not even the angels of heaven, nor the Son, but the Father only." The Lord, however, did leave us with some critical information about the events which will lead up to it.

Before we delve into the timing of the Resurrection, we need to understand who the people being resurrected are and what that event means. In our study of the Scripture it is clear that two groups of people will be resurrected, Believers and non-believers.

Daniel 12:1-2 says, "At that time shall arise Michael, the great prince who has charge of your people. And there shall be a time of trouble, such as never has been since there was a nation till that time. But at that time your people shall be delivered, everyone whose name shall be found written in the book. And many of those who sleep in the dust of the earth shall awake, some to everlasting life, and some to shame and everlasting contempt." Daniel is told that there will come a great time of trial, which we call the Tribulation, where "your people" will be delivered. The angel goes on to reveal that there are going to be *two* resurrections, where some people will be raised to everlasting life, and some to shame and everlasting contempt.

Dispensationalists love to site this passage and claim that it is speaking solely of the nation Israel. Without studying the full scope of the Scriptures it may appear to have merit, especially when you consider that "your people" suggests, at first glance, that the Prophet Daniel is only speaking about the physical descendants of Jacob. The New Testament, however, brings into focus what was only understood in the abstract; namely that, after Christ, the believing Gentiles are also considered to be " ... fellow heirs, members of the same body, and partakers of the promise in Christ Jesus through the gospel" (Ephesians 3:6).

Christ is the fulfillment of all that the Jews were waiting for, and it is through Him (and in Him) that the Gentiles have the right to partake of the promises of Abraham and become part of the commonwealth of Israel. "Therefore remember that at one time you Gentiles in the flesh, called 'the uncircumcision' by what is called the circumcision, which is made in the flesh by hands—remember that you were at that time separated from Christ, alienated from the commonwealth of Israel and strangers to the covenants of promise, having no hope and without God in the world. But now in Christ Jesus you who once were far off have been brought near by the blood of Christ" (Ephesians 2:11-13).

Paul calls this truth a *"mystery"* which was hidden in ages past but which God has now revealed. He says, "For this reason I, Paul, a prisoner for Christ Jesus on behalf of you Gentiles— assuming that you have heard of the stewardship of God's grace that was given to me for you, how the mystery was made known to me by revelation, as I have written briefly. When you read this, you can perceive my insight into the mystery of Christ, which was not made known to the sons of men in other generations as it has now been revealed to his holy apostles and prophets by the Spirit. **This mystery is that the Gentiles are fellow heirs, members of the same body, and partakers of the promise in Christ Jesus through the gospel**" (Ephesians 3:1-6; emphasis ours).

In Romans 15:8-12 Paul proclaims, "For I tell you that Christ became a servant to the circumcised to show God's truthfulness, **in order to confirm the promises given to the patriarchs,** and in order that the Gentiles might glorify God for his mercy. As it is written, 'Therefore I will praise you among the Gentiles, and sing to your name'. And again it is said, 'Rejoice, O Gentiles, with his people'. And again, 'Praise the Lord, all you Gentiles, and let the people extol him'. And again Isaiah says, 'The root of Jesse will come, even he who arises to rule the Gentiles; in him will the Gentiles hope'" (emphasis ours).

Paul elaborates this earlier, in Romans 11:16-20. Referring to the relationship between Gentiles and Jews, he says, "If the dough offered as firstfruits is holy, so is the whole lump, and if the root is holy, so are the branches. But if some of the branches were broken off, and you, although a wild olive shoot, were grafted in among the others and now share in the nourishing root of the olive tree, do not be arrogant toward the branches. If you are, remember it is not you who support the root, but the root that supports you. Then you will say, 'Branches were broken off so that I might be grafted in.' That is true. They were broken off because of their unbelief, but you stand fast through faith … "

What Dispensationalists either forget or deliberately appear to ignore is that *"the root"* is Christ, **not** Jacob and not even Abraham. It is by Him and through Him **alone** that people are grafted into God's promise. How? By faith, not by bloodline or genetic heritage.

John the Baptist even pointed this out. While baptizing in the wilderness of Judea, and seeing that the Pharisees and Sadducees were coming to be baptized also, he castigated them, warning them to bring forth " … fruit in keeping with repentance" (Matthew 3:8). He then warned them against self-righteousness because they were descendent from Abraham, saying "And do not presume to say to yourselves, 'We have Abraham as our father,' for I tell you, God is able from these stones to raise up children for Abraham" (Matthew 3:9).

What value, then, does being born a Jew or having a genetic connection to Abraham do for anyone if God can take stones and make them Abraham's children? Since it is clear that the promise comes by faith and not a result of birth, there can be no value in the flesh, meaning that the most zealous and sincere Jew faces the same choice as the most moral atheist: they will either be saved by grace alone through faith alone in Christ alone, or they will be eternally condemned to the Lake of Fire.

The Jews were *"broken off"* because Christ, a Jew by birth and physical heritage (through Mary) came to them as promised, and they rejected him. They, who, by the flesh, could count themselves the children of Abraham through Isaac and Jacob, and who felt they had a special dispensation (but trusted in the works of the flesh rather than faith), were told it mattered nothing, because they did not accept the promise by faith (Romans 9:31-32).

The Gentiles, on the other hand, could not be the children of Abraham by flesh and were, therefore, outside of the promises given to Israel. They were, as the Bible says, a "wild olive shoot" and not part of the natural tree. Yet God, in his mercy, grafts Believers into the tree and makes them partakers of His covenant, and the heirs of Abraham (His children, in effect, see Romans 9:26). Why? Because, like him, they believed by *faith* alone. In this way, they have been grafted into the tree of Israel and the promises accorded the natural branches that grew out of it (i.e. those born of the family of Abraham through Isaac and, finally, Jacob) are now accorded to them because of their faith in Christ who is, Himself, the very root of the tree.

This means (however hard it may be to hear or even understand) that non-Christian Jews, like all non-Christians, have no right to the promises granted Abraham. Much as Esau traded his birthright for stew, so have those born into the family that began with Abraham rejected their birthright when they rejected faith in Christ (Hebrews 12:16-17, Romans 9:13).

Salvation, and the promises associated with it, is not like an heirloom. It cannot be passed down from generation to generation; it has to be received through the agency of a personal act of faith in Jesus Christ. There is, therefore, no difference between Jews, Muslims, or Atheists in the eyes of God since all these are outside of the covenant founded in the blood sacrifice at Calvary for sinners. To suggest otherwise — to pretend that there is some kind of special dispensation for those who are born Jewish — is a slap in the face to God because such claims put physical lineage of birth over the physical death of Jesus, and makes the flesh of Abraham superior to the faith of Abraham.

Being a physical descendant, therefore, is meaningless. In Christ, *all* are called the children of Abraham *and* the children of God. This is what Christ came to accomplish. He took down the middle wall of partition so Jews and Gentiles could be joint heirs and children of the kingdom.

Explaining this truth further, Paul says Abraham " ... received the sign of circumcision as a seal of the righteousness that he had by faith while he was still uncircumcised. The purpose was to make him the father of all who believe without being circumcised, so that the righteousness would be counted to them as well, and to make him the father of the circumcised, who are not merely circumcised but who also walk in the footsteps of the faith that our father Abraham had before he was circumcised. For the promise to Abraham and his offspring that he would be heir of the world did not come through the law but through the righteousness of faith" (Romans 4:11-13).

The Scriptures say that Abraham is the father of all who believe, whether they are of the Circumcision (Jews) or of the Uncircumcision (Gentiles). It also says that the promise of being an heir of Abraham was through the righteousness of faith when he believed God and left his own country and followed Him into a new land. Therefore the true descendants of Abraham are not those through the flesh, but through the "offspring," and that "offspring" is Christ (Galatians 3:16).

To be in Christ (and a decedent of Abraham) requires faith in Him. Since Christ is the "offspring" of Abraham, the only way to be an heir of Abraham must also be through faith. Thus anyone boasting of a physical link has nothing to brag about, for that does not give them automatic access into the Kingdom (as

John the Baptist explained), or assures them of special treatment when the Lord returns to establish his Kingdom at the end of the Tribulation.

In light of this tremendous truth is it any wonder there is no mention made of the Gentile believers in Daniel's prophecy? The words he spoke, concerning the prophecy given him, were a "mystery," which Paul (speaking hundreds of years later) explained to the Church at Ephesus (Ephesians 3:6). It was prophesied in the Old Testament, but had to wait until its fulfillment after Christ, even though there were examples in the Old Testament of what was to take place in the New Testament in believing Gentiles like Rahab, Ruth, Uriah the Hittite and others.

These individuals fulfilled what was spoken of in Exodus 12:48-49, which says, "If a stranger shall sojourn with you, and would keep the Passover to the LORD, let all his males be circumcised. Then he may come near and keep it; **he shall be as a native of the land**. But no uncircumcised person shall eat of it. There shall be one law for the native and for the stranger who sojourns among you" (emphasis ours). So even in the Old Testament we see that there was a provision for Gentiles to be grafted into the body, whereas now we see this truth fully developed in the New Testament epistles.

This understanding in no way takes away from what the angel is telling Daniel because when he speaks of Daniel's "people" (Daniel 12) he is not focused strictly on the Jewish inhabitants of ancient Israel, but all who are elect and chosen of God for salvation. There has always been the elect within the visible body (Romans 9:25-27; 11:1-7).

Some think this is a revolutionary idea. Dispensationalists, in fact, label these ideas as 'Replacement Theology.' Replacement Theology is the idea that the Church somehow 'replaces' Israel and becomes the inheritors of the promises made to Abraham. This is because Dispensationalists, having determined that a division exists between Israel and the Church, are concerned about the Church taking the promises which they believe were given to the Jews.

We are, however, like our brother Charles Haddon Spurgeon and many of the Puritans and Reformers not averse to calling the Church "the Israel of God." We do this because the Apostle Paul did it in Galatians 6:15-16: "For neither circumcision counts for anything, nor uncircumcision, but a new creation. And as for all who walk by this rule, peace and mercy be upon them, and upon the Israel of God."

By labeling this doctrine Replacement Theology the Dispensationalist implies that it carries with it the stigma and accusation of either 'not taking the Bible literally' or of deliberately twisting its meaning. Our response to them is that if you accuse us of this, you must also accuse Paul.

It was Paul, not us, who says, " ... the Gentiles are fellow heirs, members **of the same body**, and partakers of the promise in Christ Jesus through the gospel" (Ephesians 3:6; emphasis ours). If Gentile Christians are the "same body" as believing Jews, and have the promises given Abraham through Christ by salvation, what is the value of being Jewish or an Israelite in this present time? There is none, for if salvation is dependent on genealogy it is not of faith. And if being born a Jew has some equivalent value to faith in Christ, you effectively nullify the suffering and sacrifice of Jesus and go against what the Bible says in Acts 4:12: " ... there is no other name under heaven given among men by which we must be saved."

Non-Christian Jews, like non-Christians everywhere, are *not* entitled to the promises of Abraham *because they are not saved.* Since they are not in Christ, they are also **not** Daniel's "*people*." Daniel's people were not the entire nation of Israel but the elect within Israel. So, when Paul explains that Gentile Believers are "fellow heirs, members of the same body" that means they have been *grafted*, spiritually, **into** the body of the faithful Jews and thus ***coequal*** heirs of the promises granted Abraham and his descendants. The unfaithful Jew or Gentile has nothing and will only partake of God's eternal wrath and judgement.

It also goes against the principle of understanding and interpreting Scripture with Scripture, and not via the vague notions and wild understanding taught by those whose eschatology demands a selective insight and interpretation of the Bible. Only by taking the entirety of what the Bible clearly says, and putting it together based on the understanding that Christ is at the center of *all* Scripture, can anyone truly discern what God is communicating.

The Bible is *not* two books but one. It is not primarily a story about the Jews and the Gentiles, or about Israel and non-Israel. It is the story of a fallen world and God's plan to reconcile it to Himself. So when Daniel is told that two groups of people will be resurrected,

"... some to everlasting life, and some to shame and everlasting contempt" (Daniel 12:2), he is not speaking about events that will encompass Israel and the Jews alone, but the whole of humanity.

This is explained further by the Apostle John, who in Revelation 20:5 says, "The rest of the dead did not come to life until the thousand years were ended. This is the first resurrection." Verses 11-15 of the same chapter say, "Then I saw a great white throne and him who was seated on it. From his presence earth and sky fled away, and no place was found for them. And I saw the dead, great and small, standing before the throne, and books were opened. Then another book was opened, which is the book of life. And the dead were judged by what was written in the books, according to what they had done. And the sea gave up the dead who were in it, Death and Hades gave up the dead who were in them, and they were judged, each one of them, according to what they had done. Then Death and Hades were thrown into the lake of fire. This is the second death, the lake of fire. And if anyone's name was not found written in the book of life, he was thrown into the lake of fire."

The "first resurrection" and the second resurrection described by John are the two groups Daniel spoke about. The first group are those that are either alive when Christ returns after the Tribulation or who had died in Christ beforehand. The latter group is resurrected to face God's wrath after the thousand-year (or Millennial) reign of Christ.

Christ himself confirms this when He says, " ... for an hour is coming when all who are in the tombs shall hear his voice and come out, those who have done good to the resurrection of life, and those who have done evil to the resurrection of judgement" (John 5:28-29).

Revelation 20:7 says, "And when the thousand years were ended, Satan will be released ... " and then the events which follow lead to the great white throne judgement. But when will *the first resurrection* happen? This is explained in Revelation 19:11-13 which says, "Then I saw heaven opened, and behold a white horse! The one sitting on it is called Faithful and True, and in righteousness he judges and makes war. His eyes are like a flame of fire, and on his head are many diadems, and he has a name written that no one knows but himself. He is clothed in a robe dipped in blood, and the name by which he is called is The Word of God."

This is the portrait of Christ's return that John has painted for us. He goes on to explain the details of the climactic events which will take place at His coming, such as the war which ensues upon His arrival as He slaughters the wicked, the Beast and False Prophet captured and tossed into the Lake of Fire, and Satan bound for a thousand years. It is at this point, at the beginning of the next chapter of Revelation, that the Rapture, or *the first resurrection*, takes place.

In Revelation 20:1-3, John explains that the Devil is captured and thrown into the bottomless pit. *After* that event, he tells us that he " ... saw thrones, and seated on them were those to whom the authority to judge was committed. Also I saw the souls of those who had been beheaded for the testimony of Jesus and for the word of God, and those who had not worshipped the beast or its image and had not received its mark on their foreheads or their hands. They came to life and reigned with Christ for a thousand years" (Revelation 20:4) Then, in verse 5 we read, "The rest of the dead did not come to life until the thousand years were ended. This is **the first resurrection**" (emphasis ours). From these passages it is clear that *"the first resurrection"* happens when Christ returns in

" … flaming fire, inflicting vengeance on those who do not know God … " (2 Thessalonians 1:8).

Some will say that this verse only applies to those saints who have perished during the Tribulation period, otherwise known as Tribulation Saints, because Revelation 20:5 occurs after the supposed Pre-Trib Rapture and marks the end of the Tribulation. The irony, of course, is that *this* resurrection does take place *after* the Tribulation, thus making it (if Dispensational logic is followed) not "the first resurrection" but the second; the "first" and invisible and sudden one having occurred on the eve of the Tribulation according to Dispensational thought.

1 Thessalonians 4:16-17 is the verse some people site as proof of there being a Pre-tribulation Rapture. Yet, if taken literally, as Dispensationalists say they do, then John is mistaken when he places "the first resurrection" at the end of the Tribulation (meaning there was no rising of the dead or even living believers before it).

What then becomes of the event in Revelation 20:13? This resurrection takes place *after* the end of the Christ-ruled Millennium, at the Great White Throne judgement, when those not blessed to take part in *"the first resurrection"* are raised up. If the Dispensationalists are to be believed, this would then constitute a ***third*** resurrection and not the second.

Admittedly, John does not specifically mention that the Saints of old will be raised up along with Christian believers in Revelation 20:5 ("the first resurrection"), although this hardly validates the view that this event covers only those who died during the Tribulation, nor does it mean they are excluded. By using the definite article *"**the**"* before *"**first resurrection**"* John is categorically saying that no event similar to this occurred beforehand; that it is ***the first***. Now if this is the first, why would God allow the prophets and holy people of old to wait until the second, where those not blessed are raised up? Clearly when *the first resurrection* occurs ***all*** the saints of God, from both New and Old Testament times, will be taken up as well and reign with Christ a thousand years upon the Earth.

John says that Christ has made us " ... a kingdom, priests to his God and Father ..." (Revelation 1:6). He also says, referring to the saints in Heaven, that they have been made " ... a kingdom and priests to our God, and they shall reign on the earth." (Revelation 5:10). Even the man most strongly credited with spreading

Dispensationalism to the masses (and, consequently, the Pre-Trib Rapture view), Dr. C.I. Schofield, in his book, 'The Word of Truth Rightly Divided,' finds no fault with this position.

Schofield wrote, " ... After the purifying judgements which attend the personal return of Christ to the earth, He will reign over restored Israel and over the earth for one thousand years. This is the period commonly called the Millennium. The seat of His power will be Jerusalem, and the saints, including the saved of the Dispensation of Grace, viz., the Church, will be associated with Him in His glory ..."[85]

This is an incredible statement and shows just how weak the case for the Pre-Trib Rapture is. If, even according to Scofield, " ... the saints, including the saved of the Dispensation of Grace, viz., the Church, will be associated with Him in His glory ... " (presumably "the saints" prior to "the Dispensation of Grace" are the faithful people in Old Testament times) it, effectively undermines the view that Revelation 20:5 speaks only about the 'Trib Saints.' If it doesn't, then you not only have a different dispensation for the Jews and the Church, but

---

[85] C.I. Scofield, The Word of Truth Rightly Divided, pg. 18.

now you have yet another dispensation between the saints raptured and/or resurrected before the Tribulation, and those resurrected after it.

This, again, is not Dispensationalism, it is what we earlier referred to as "missed the bus theology" where those who are saved before the Tribulation are considered more worthy of reigning with Christ than those who will have to suffer and die during this horrible period. But if they are not part of the Church, and hence the body of Christ, how can they be counted worthy of being spared from the second death? This view is clearly unscriptural and can only be derived through the distortion effects of reading the Bible through Dispensational lenses.

The cure for this is a careful study of Daniel, and other portions of the Scriptures, in order to understand the full scope of what Revelation 20:5 is teaching. This verse is critical to debunking the entire Dispensational argument for the Pre-Tribulation Rapture theory. It is the stumbling block that causes people like LaHaye and others to invent ideas about *the first resurrection* taking place in 'phases' in order to make it line up with their eschatological views. Yet ignorance of the passage is also what makes possible the bizarre notion that there are separate dispensations for the Jews and the

Gentiles, and why some people believe that certain Christians will reign with Him and others will not. It is the breeding ground, in fact, for fallacies such as the exultation of Judaism, and imputing to it a spiritual equality with Christianity that it does not possess Biblically.

Regarding the idea of the Rapture or *the first resurrection* taking place in phases, in chapter five we mentioned our e-mail correspondence with Rev. Todd Baker and how he tried to provide a logical explanation for his view. He failed, and miserably so. Why? It's not that Baker is not an intelligent man or a heretic. In fact, from our correspondence with him, he appears to be a fine and upstanding Christian, with a lot of gifts and a desire to save souls.

Despite this, and like many other Christians in his camp, Reverend Baker is so steeped in his eschatology that any contrary scripture-based view is hard to accept. If they do —if they even venture to consider that *the first resurrection* (and hence the Rapture) happens at the end of the Tribulation as Scripture says it does—it messes up their entire system and throws into doubt teachings that are almost 200 years old.

This is not a small or an easy thing to do. Millions of Christians have been taught, from their earliest days, that the Rapture will remove them before the terrible events of the last days take place. Seminaries and universities, PhD's, and common lay people in essentially solid, fundamentalist, Protestant Evangelical churches throughout the world know nothing but this view. Yet it is built on a wrong understanding of Scripture just the same and needs to be corrected.

Now consider Jesus' own teaching on the resurrection. When he went to the house of Mary and Martha after their brother Lazarus had died, Martha said to Jesus, " ... Lord, if you had been here, my brother would not have died. But even now I know that whatever you ask from God, God will give you. Jesus said to her, 'Your brother will rise again'" (John 11:21-23). What is Martha's response to this? Having no idea that the Lord was speaking about resurrecting their brother right away, she replied, " ... I know that he will rise again in the resurrection on the last day" (John 11:24). She didn't say she had confidence that Lazarus would rise at the Pre-Trib Rapture, or, the first *phase* of the resurrection. She said it would happen at "the resurrection on the last day." How much clearer could the Bible have stated this?

Now, some would say she did not *know* about the Pre-Trib rapture since the Revelation of John did not come until later. This argument, however, is very disingenuous because it presupposes that the Pre-Trib rapture view existed in the earliest days of the Church in some form; which, as we have shown, is wrong, it having begun only about 200 years ago with John Nelson Darby.

This either makes Martha ignorant or, at best, misinformed. Yet it is, nonetheless, interesting that Christ made no attempt to change her point of view. Thus it can be believed that there would only be one resurrection for Believers, the one to which Martha, Christ, and John, along with Matthew and Mark (who wrote of Christ's debate with the Sadducees regarding the Resurrection in Matthew 22:23-33, and Mark 12:28-27) were referring to, and not two or three, or one that takes place in phases.

In another instance Jesus disputed with the Pharisees about how He truly is the bread of life saying, "For I have come down from heaven, not to do my own will but the will of him who sent me. And this is the will of him who sent me, that I should lose nothing of all that he has given me, but raise it up on the last day" (John 6:38-39). Again, Christ said "the last day." This is not the "last day before the Pre-Trib rapture," nor is it the last day where the second resurrection occurs and the wicked will be brought before the Great White Throne for judgement. This then has to occur at Christ's physical coming in glory.

Dispensationalists, however, cannot or will not see it in this light because (to our understanding) it does not fit into their system of theology. Not willing to abandon their cherished dream of avoiding the Tribulation they proceed by clever devices such as breaking "the last day" and "the first resurrection" into phases in order to *make* it fit.

Scripture, however, is clear and if taken in its plain sense reveals that there are only two resurrections—the first to eternal life which happens *after* the Tribulation (Revelation 20:5-6), and the second to eternal damnation and happens after the thousand-year reign of Christ with His saints (Revelation 20:7-15).

The prophet Daniel spoke of two general resurrections. He wrote: "And many of those who sleep in the dust of the earth shall awake, some to everlasting life, and some to shame and everlasting contempt" (Daniel 12:2). The Apostle Paul also confirmed this truth when he was speaking before Felix and said, " … having a hope in God … that there will be a resurrection of both the just and the unjust" (Acts 24:15).

To say there are phases to "the first resurrection" leaves open the Dispensationalist to charges of spiritualizing what does not agree with their eschatology and mocks their claim of having a monopoly on the literal interpretation of Scripture. Moreover, it does not do justice to the Word of God and must be abandoned.

9

The Matthew 24 Controversy

Since the rise of Dispensationalism, a huge chasm has developed in the way they, and those who hold to Reformed theology, interpret Matthew 24. Even within Reformed circles there are disagreements with certain aspects of this chapter, but they are not as severe as those disagreements with the Dispensationalists.

Matthew 24 describes many prophetic events that will come to pass. In it Christ answers three key questions posed by the disciples concerning the end time. These are: "…

when will these things be, and what will be the sign of your coming and of the close of the age?" (Matthew 24:3)

These questions came about from a statement Jesus had made concerning what was to happen to the Temple at a future time. The Bible says, "Jesus left the temple and was going away, when his disciples came to point out to him the buildings of the temple. But he answered them, 'You see all these, do you not? Truly, I say to you, there will not be left here one stone upon another that will not be thrown down'" (Matthew 24:1-2).

The beauty of the Temple and all its glory may have enamoured His disciples, as it no doubt enamoured most in ancient Judea. It was the place where God had appointed that, until Christ's death, the shadows of His New Covenant should be manifested in the sacrifices which took place there. Christ also knew, that like other works made by the hand of man, it was temporary, and was to exist until His manifestation in the flesh.

Yet what's interesting about this whole exchange is that Jesus did not mention that the events He was describing were going to take place at His Second Coming. His disciples, however, understood that the event Christ was recounting could only happen at that time because it was only then that the end of the world would occur. What they wanted to know was *when* it was going to happen, *what signs* were going to accompany Christ's return, and *when* the end of the world was.

Earlier we mentioned how the Dispensationalists love to claim a virtual monopoly on the literal method of Biblical interpretation, and, therefore, only their interpretations are valid. Stanton says, "It is generally safe to assume that when two passages of Scripture, although similar, fail to agree in their important points, that they are speaking of different events and possibly concern different peoples ... "[86] He goes on to say that he is specifically speaking about Matthew 24 and 1 Thessalonians 4:13-18. He says, " ... dispensationalists hold that Matthew 24 speaks of Israel in the Tribulation and not of the Church, which they believe to be already raptured (possibly between the eighth and the ninth verses of this chapter). They hold that I Thessalonians 4:13-18 is the primary passage which deals with the rapture of the Church, and

---

[86] Gerald B. Stanton, Kept From the Hour: Biblical Evidence for the Pretribulational Return of Christ, pg. 56.

that Matthew 24 describes a different event and a different people, namely, the revelation of Christ in respect to Israel following the Tribulation ... "[87]

How does he come to this conclusion? Through Dispensationalism of course! Stanton says, "Seeking to harmonize the Scriptures and to apply to Israel and to the Church those things which particularly pertain to each, many Bible students have employed interpretive principles which have come to be called 'dispensationalism' ... "[88]

From this example it is clear that the Dispensational theological system is merely derived from their interpretation of Scripture and not the literal method as they believe. Of course they claim that Dispensationalism actually arose from a literal understanding of the Scriptures themselves, but that is clearly not the case.

For them everything they believe is built on the idea that there is a virtual and complete separation of the things (blessings and events) ordained by God for Israel and the Church. This

---

[87] Ibid. pg. 57

[88] Ibid. pg. 56-57

goes against the fact that Christ represents, in total, the fulfillment of all the promises given to Abraham.

The Scriptures say, "That is why it depends on faith, in order that the promise may rest on grace and be guaranteed to all his offspring—not only to the adherent of the law but also to the one who shares the faith of Abraham, who is the father of us all, as it is written, 'I have made you the father of many nations'—in the presence of the God in whom he believed, who gives life to the dead and calls into existence the things that do not exist. In hope he believed against hope, that he should become the father of many nations, as he had been told, 'So shall your offspring be.'" (Romans 4:16-18). Where many Dispensationalists make their error is by saying that the "seed" are the physical descendants of Israel (Israel, in this case, referring to Jacob, the son of Isaac, the son of Abraham) and are, therefore, the true inheritors of the promises given to Abraham. But Paul points out in Galatians 3:16-29 that the "seed" is really Christ, and it is only through Him, and by Him, alone, that salvation is given.

Paul says that in Christ "There is neither Jew nor Greek, there is neither slave nor free, there is no male and female, for you are all one in Christ Jesus. And if you are Christ's, then you are Abraham's offspring, heirs according to promise." (Galatians 3:28-29). He repeats this same thought in Ephesians where he says, "remember that you were at that time separated from Christ, alienated from the commonwealth of Israel and strangers to the covenants of promise, having no hope and without God in the world. But now in Christ Jesus you who once were far off have been brought near by the blood of Christ" (Ephesians 2:12-13).

The promises given to Abraham were not to be fulfilled according to the flesh or the law itself, but through his faith in God. Genesis 15:6 says, Abram " ... believed the LORD, and he counted it to him as righteousness." This promise was given before the covenant of circumcision, meaning that Abram (before he was called Abraham) was considered righteous by God simply because he had faith in Him; something which Paul affirms in Ephesians 2:8-11 and Galatians 3:14-16.

Circumcision was the sign of the covenant that pledged Abraham, and his physical descendants, to the Lord until Christ should appear and make this symbol unnecessary. It was the outward sign of the covenant which was to represent the inward reality of having their hearts circumcised (Deuteronomy 10:16; 30:6; Jeremiah 4:4; Romans 2:29).

The reality of the matter is that the unsaved Jews of our time are no more saved than are Muslims, Buddhists, or atheists. They might have the works of the Law. They might even have the form of Godliness found in them and perform them as much as is in their power. But NONE of these works can save them because salvation is by grace alone through faith alone in Christ alone (Ephesians 2:8, 9; Acts 16:31).

Romans 3:20-22 says: "For by the works of the law no human being will be justified in his sight, since through the law comes knowledge of sin. But now the righteousness of God has been manifested apart from the law, although the Law and Prophets bear witness to it—the righteousness of God through faith in Jesus Christ for all who believe. For there is no distinction." It also says, in Galatians 3:23-25: "Now before faith came, we were held captive under the law, imprisoned until the coming faith would be revealed. So then, the law was our guardian (or schoolmaster) until Christ came, in order that we might be justified by faith. But now that faith has come, we are no longer under a guardian."

A person becomes an heir of Abraham, and thus a partaker of the promises handed down from him and through the 12 patriarchs unto Christ, not because he is a Jew or identifies with Judaism, but because he believes in God through faith alone in Christ alone. If it were otherwise, then it would effectively nullify the sacrifice of Christ, which was not a sacrifice given for the Gentiles alone, but for all people who believe in Him by faith.

Without Jesus, therefore (without "the seed"), there can be no reconciliation with God. And without that reconciliation the only inheritance is of eternal damnation.

Dispensationalists like to refer to this (as we mentioned previously), derogatorily, as 'Replacement Theology' whereby the Christian Church 'takes over' the blessings granted to Abraham. Implicit in their disparagement, of course, is that this 'taking over' is unbiblical because of their notion of a separation between spiritual blessings and earthly blessings; between one body and another; between Israel (the land and physical descendants of Jacob) and the Church (the Believers). But, once again, they fail to understand that the blessings are spiritual in origin and spiritual in application.

When God gave the promises to Abraham, He told him to " ... 'Look toward heaven, and number the stars, if you are able to number them.' Then he said to him, 'So shall your offspring be.' And he believed the LORD, and he counted it to him as righteousness" (Genesis 15:5-6).

Did God mean *only* the descendants of his body? How could he? *If* that were the case, no Gentile could possibly be saved, regardless of what Christ did, and salvation would be only for the Jews. Yet it was largely the Jews that rejected Him and the Gentiles who received Him.

Granted, the first Believers were all Jews until God poured out the Spirit upon Cornelius and his friends and family while Peter preached to them (Acts 10). There are also many Jewish-born Believers today. But compared to the numbers of Christians today, they are relatively few.

Who, then, are the descendants of Abraham? Who are the chosen people? Even Ishmael, Abraham's first born through his handmaid Hagar, is considered his son and the descendants through him (the Arabs) count him as their Patriarch. Are they to be partakers of the eternal blessings granted Abraham based on that?

The Arabs presently outnumber the population of the State of Israel and the worldwide Diaspora of Jews by several dozen times; so much so that they can barely be numbered. Are these Arab descendants of Abraham not entitled to the promises made him simply based on their numbers? If they were, then the will of the flesh would have power over the will of God; for the Lord says, "And as for Ishmael, I have heard you; behold, I have blessed him and will make him fruitful and multiply him greatly. He shall father twelve princes, and I will make him into a great nation. **But I will establish my covenant with Isaac, whom Sarah shall bear to you at this time next year.**" (Genesis 17:20-21; emphasis ours).

The Lord had decided to establish Abraham's line, and hence the inheritance, through Isaac, and then Jacob his son, who passed it on to the twelve tribes of Israel, and ultimately to the 'seed' which is Christ. If the seed is Christ, as we mentioned above, and Christ Himself had no physical descendants, how then can the promise be obtained by anyone?

It can only be done by faith alone; not the 'faith' that one is a descendant of Abraham, Isaac, and Jacob. Not the false 'faith' that one is tied to the promises through physical association with Ishmael, but by faith in Christ alone.

Thus it is not those who are born Jews or the physical descendants of Israel who are the true heirs of the Abrahamic promises but those who believe in Jesus, Jews and Gentiles alike. And while the Church or Christ's body may not be Israel physically, it is to them, and only them, to whom belong the promises.

This is not Replacement Theology nor is it God abandoning, in any way, His covenant with Israel. It is, rather, Fulfillment Theology; the view that those promises and covenants are. will be, and were *fulfilled* in Jesus Christ, whose death, resurrection, and return will bring a close to our present age.

Stanton, however, spends a great deal of time in his book attempting to prove the opposite. To him, and others like him, the verses he uses suggest that they are really speaking about different events and concern different people. They don't, but that doesn't stop him from trying to prove otherwise.

That is the single greatest blind spot Dispensationalists have; instead of taking the Scriptures literally (as they claim they do) they twist them to fit their theological system. In the process, they end up trying to *prove* something that agrees with their preconceived ideas rather than what the Scriptures actually teach.

For example, in 1 Thessalonians 4:13-18, the apostle Paul is describing *how* the resurrection takes place, while Jesus, in His discourse in Matthew 24, explains the *entire scope* of His second coming.

There is no contradiction here, nor are their two different events, affecting two different peoples in view. You also don't need Dispensationalism to 'reconcile' these passages with each other in order to see how they fit. In short, there's nothing to reconcile. They speak for themselves.

Stanton, on the other hand, says, "A direct comparison between Matthew 24 and I Thessalonians 4 will strengthen the conviction that two different events are in view ..."[89] He then proceeds to describe these differences by telling his readers that, "The terminology is not the same. Matthew 24 speaks of the sign of the Son of Man, the name Christ commonly used in his earthly relationships, but in I Thessalonians 4, it is "the Lord himself."[90]

---

[89] Gerald B. Stanton, Kept From the Hour: Biblical Evidence for the Pretribulational Return of Christ, pg. 62.

[90] Ibid.

To Stanton, the fact that Christ refers to Himself as the Son of Man in one place, while Paul calls Him "the Lord himself" in another somehow justifies his view that these are two different events. Yet Christ has many names which are applied to him in several passages throughout the Scripture. Nonetheless, these names cannot be *assumed* to mean two different applications of Christ's end-time role, nor can such minor distinctions be used to justify an eschatological position completely at odds with the plain reading of the text.

That, of course, does not stop Stanton from trying. In fact, for the Dispensationalist, such hair-splitting is key to their self-proclaimed and self-justified view of being the guardians of the literal interpretation.

But, looking at it without imposing Dispensational ideas on the passage, one can clearly see, in his letter to the Thessalonians, that Paul was actually *explaining* the events of the resurrection and reassuring them of the Lord's coming, lest they believe their loved ones are dead forever. He says, "Therefore encourage one another with these words" (1 Thessalonians 4:18).

What can be of greater comfort to one's spirit and heart than knowing that "the Lord himself" will be descending in order to resurrect us all? In fact, less would be the comfort had Paul told the Thessalonians that the supposed Pre-trib Rapture was specific to only one group of people, or that the event would take place at an hour they did not expect with no signs preceding it, as Pre-tribbers insist with their doctrine of immanency.

That, of course, means nothing to Stanton who continues in his reasoning by saying, "In Matthew, there are signs in the heavens, the sun and the moon refusing to shine, the stars falling, and the powers of heavens shaken. These are in keeping with the Jewish content of the passage, for the Jews are a 'sign people' (1 Cor. 1:22); however, one looks in vain for such signs and marvels in the 1 Thessalonians passage."[91]

Again, Stanton seems to miss it. He refuses to see that Christ is detailing the time leading up to his coming, while Paul is focused on explaining the resurrection of Believers. As for Stanton's comment that the Jews are a 'sign people,' he fails to recognize that Paul is making a reference to the encounter Christ had with the Pharisees when they asked a sign from Him in Matthew 16. Neither Jesus, nor Paul, were

---

[91] Ibid.

pointing out some kind of cultural characteristic that they could be proud of, but both were condemning their unfaithfulness in that they had the scriptures, which prophesied the events of Christ's ministry, and *still* wanted to see 'signs' in order to verify what was plainly in front of them.

Paul says, "For Jews demand signs and Greeks seek wisdom, but we preach Christ crucified, a stumbling block to Jews and folly to Gentiles, but to those who are called, both Jews and Greeks, Christ the power of God and the wisdom of God" (1 Corinthians 1:22-24). But what was the 'sign' the Jews required? Was it concerning the events, which are laid out in Matthew 24 as Stanton, and others claim? We do not believe so.

In Matthew 16:2-4 Jesus tells the Pharisees and Sadducees, who came to Him seeking a sign in order to tempt him, " ... When it is evening you say, 'It will be fair weather, for the sky is red.' And in the morning, 'It will be stormy today, for the sky is red and threatening.' You know how to interpret the appearance of the sky, but you cannot interpret the signs of the times. An evil and adulterous generation seeks for a sign, but no sign will be given to it except the sign of Jonah ... "

These people were actually demanding Christ perform some miraculous sign from Heaven (just as Elijah did), when the reality of the situation was that they had failed to detect the foretold season and time of His coming. If they were truly wise, they would have known (through the study of the prophets) that Christ had come to fulfill what was written. They had the ministry of John the Baptist preaching in the wilderness; they had Jesus Himself fulfilling all of the prophesied healings and miracles; they had the angels announcing His birth; they heard His wisdom and truth, and many more events which circled around His life to prove that they were living in the *season* of the Messiah's coming.

The same holds true of the signs spoken of in Matthew 24 concerning His Second Coming. In this passage Jesus explicitly states the events which will herald His return in glory. If His return were to be a secret one, involving an unexpected rapture of the faithful, there would be little point to announcing it to His disciples beforehand. It would also defy logic since there is no way to expect an unexpected event; the minute you tell someone to expect the unexpected they begin to live in expectation.

There would also be little point in making the astounding claim that He said this specifically for the sake of the Jews. At that time all of the disciples were Jews, but to state that Matthew 24 only applies to them also defies logic since Jews reject faith in Christ and hence are not likely to read this passage in the first place. It would be like preparing dinner, inviting people to eat, but then telling those that arrived that the food was only for those who would not show up.

How can Stanton then claim that these passages are to be seen " ... in keeping with the Jewish content of the passage ... ?" The only content is the literal one, where Jesus explains to His followers the events leading up to His return, which were for everyone who believes in Him.

Yet Stanton continues to try to reconcile 1 Thessalonians with Matthew 24, saying, "In Matthew, there are judgements, warnings of Antichrist, and instructions for escape; in the Thessalonians passage, judgement is not found, Antichrist is not in view, and provision for escape is not mentioned for it is not needed."[92] That argument is equally absurd and comes

---

[92] Ibid.

straight out of the Dispensational view that 'escape' is the goal and not endurance of the Tribulation. Like a poor artist, he had drawn the picture beforehand, and now wants to alter the model or the object to fit it, instead of doing it the proper way around.

Stanton's reasoning is fundamentally flawed. Had he realized that Christ was explaining the events leading up to His Second Advent, and that Paul was explaining *how* the resurrection is to take place, he might have come to a different understanding of end-time events. As it stands, however, he merely parrots the Dispensational party-line.

Stanton's claim that, " ... in the Thessalonians passage, judgement is not found" is equally fallacious. In fact, Paul says, "Now concerning the times and the seasons, brothers, you have no need to have anything written to you. For you yourselves are fully aware that the day of the Lord will come like a thief in the night. While people are saying, 'There is peace and security,' then sudden destruction will come upon them as labor pains come upon a pregnant woman, and they will not escape" (1 Thessalonians 5:1-3).

Dispensationalists will, no doubt, refute this claim by saying that Paul is now explaining about the Tribulation *after* the Church has been raptured. They come to this conclusion by stating that verse 9 of this chapter says, " ... God has not destined us for wrath, but to obtain salvation through our Lord Jesus Christ." To them, the "wrath" spoken of in this verse is the wrath that is poured out upon the Earth during the Tribulation because they are looking to escape this time of trouble via their supposed Pre-trib Rapture.

What they fail to consider, however, is that, in the context of the Bible (never mind the context of the passage) the "wrath" God speaks of is His divine eternal wrath, which is poured out upon those who do not believe in Christ. As for the wrath of man, Christ told His disciples, before His arrest and crucifixion, " ... In the world you will have tribulation. But take heart; I have overcome the world" (John 16:33). Moreover, Jesus also warns the Church of Smyrna, in regard to their upcoming persecution, "Do not fear what you are about to suffer. Behold, the devil is about to throw some of you into prison, that you may be tested, and for ten days you will have tribulation. Be faithful unto death, and I will give you the crown of life" (Revelations 2:10).

These passages are hardly comforting to those who wish to escape the Tribulation. They may even argue that these verses are specifically directed against the disciples or the Smyrnan Believers, although, to do so would be to make light of the sufferings endured by Paul and the Apostles, including their flocks, at the hands of the Romans in the early Christian era. Moreover, it would go against what Jesus taught when He said, " … 'A servant is not greater than his master.' If they persecuted me, they will also persecute you … " (John 15:20).

It is thus clear that the idea of suffering is not an alien quality to Christendom but a condition of it. Dispensationalists, however, would have you believe that God has appointed one generation to not see this at the hands of man. But to prove this they have to violently torque the meaning of 1 Corinthians 15:51-52, in which Paul tells us that, " … We shall not all sleep, but we shall all be changed," at " … the last trumpet … "

This, in no way, suggests that those who are alive during the Tribulation will escape suffering or persecution. It does say, however, that through the providence of God, these survivors will be spared the sight of death itself at the hands of their enemies in this period.

When? At "the last trump," at the end of the Tribulation when Christ Jesus returns. Not before and not in some hoped-for Pre-trib Rapture, but after.

As for the timing of the event itself, Paul explains that it could not " ... surprise you like a thief. For you are all children of light, children of the day. We are not of the night or of the darkness. So then let us not sleep, as others do, but let us keep awake and be sober" (1 Thessalonians 5:4-6). This destroys the idea of an unanticipated, anticipated, at-any-time event which was made light of earlier.

It would also mock the need for Paul to tell the church to "keep awake and be sober." If the Church has been raptured before the Tribulation, what is there left to watch for? If it has not, again, how can you watch for an event that Dispensationalists believe you cannot know or anticipate?

Clearly only those who are in the dark about the Second Advent are the ones who will not be watching, whereas those "children of light" are watching, because they know their redemption draws near. He explains this in 1 Thessalonians 5:8-9, "But since we belong to the day, let us be sober, having put on the breastplate of faith and love, and for a helmet the hope of salvation. For God has not destined us for wrath, but to obtain salvation through our Lord Jesus Christ."

All of this points to the fact that Paul is talking about eternal salvation; salvation which comes through the conversion of the soul by repenting of your sin and exercising faith toward our Lord Jesus Christ. It is the " ... hope of salvation" (verse 8); the hope of eternal salvation through our Lord Jesus Christ, and not the hope of evading the persecution to come by a Pre-trib Rapture that people should believe in Christ for! It is this hope in our divine and eternal salvation that, in turn, comforts us, as Paul says in verse 11, "Therefore encourage one another and build one another up, just as you are doing."

It should be apparent that much of Dr. Stanton's argument rests on the fact that he has failed to see that Paul and Christ were focused on explaining different aspects of the same event. That is why, for him, "The first appearing is public and involves sinners; the second is private, with no judgement, the Church alone being in view. Two classes of men are spoken of in Matthew: the Jewish elect, and the sinful nations. Two classes are mentioned in the Thessalonians passage: 'them which are asleep,' and 'we which are alive'; these together comprise the Church, and neither class corresponds to saved Jews or unsaved nations."[93]

Instead of treating Believers as one body under the grace of God, Stanton splits them in order to appease his eschatological viewpoint. This is not, however, the only time he does this. He says, "In Matthew, there is the sound of a trumpet, but it is blown by an angel; in Thessalonians, a trumpet is sounded, but it is 'the trump of God.'"[94]

It's curious that Stanton, who aspires to be biblically literal, would make such a claim, because, in reality, Matthew 24:31 says, "And he will send out his angels with a loud trumpet call, and they will gather his elect from the four winds, from one end of heaven to the other."

Does this verse say that it was an angel who blew the trumpet? Even 1 Thessalonians does not say who or what causes the trump to sound. All it says is that the trumpet is called the trump of God. In reality, we do believe that an angel does, indeed, sound the trumpet due, in part, because in Revelation the angels do sound them. Moreover, it makes sense that someone

---

[93] Ibid. pg. 63.

[94] Ibid.

other than God Himself would sound the trumpet because, in ancient times, a returning king never announced his own arrival, but reserved that honour to one of his servants.

Concerning the blast of this particular trumpet, however, let us take the two aforementioned verses (Matthew 24:31 and 1 Thessalonians 4:16) and compare them with another verse which may shed more light on what is happening. In 1 Corinthians 15 the Apostle Paul is consumed with the explanation and defence of the resurrection. In verses 51-52 he states, "Behold! I tell you a mystery. We shall not all sleep, but we shall all be changed, in a moment, in the twinkling of an eye, at **the last trumpet**. For the trumpet will sound, and the dead will be raised imperishable, and we shall be changed" (emphasis ours).

Everyone will agree that this has to be the same event which is explained in 1 Thessalonians. But why are the Dispensationalists reluctant to associate it with Matthew 24:31? The reason is clear: If they agreed to this then that would place the resurrection *after* the tribulation. The fact that this trumpet in 1 Corinthians is called "the last trump" ought to clue everyone into the realization that this is near the end. And, if this is the last trump then the one which is described in Matthew 24:31 has to be the same, because Christ is in the process of explaining the last of the Apostles questions, namely, the sign of His coming and the end of the world (Matthew 24:3).

In the Revelation, where Christ's return is pictured, there is, in fact, seven trumpets, which are apparently sounded by angels. Regarding the seventh (or last trumpet) the Bible says: "Then the seventh angel blew his trumpet, and there were loud voices in heaven, saying, 'The kingdom of the world has become the kingdom of our Lord and of his Christ, and he shall reign forever and ever.' And the twenty-four elders who sit on their thrones before God fell on their faces and worshipped God, saying, 'We give thanks to you, Lord God Almighty, who is and who was, for you have taken your great power and begun to reign. The nations raged, but your wrath came, and the time for the dead to be judged, and for rewarding your servants, the prophets and saints, and those who fear your name, both small and great ... '" (Revelation 11:15-18).

The text tells us that at the seventh trumpet several things happen: Christ becomes King of all the kingdoms of the earth, the wicked are physically judged and destroyed at

Armageddon because they stand opposed to the arrival of the King of Kings (not to be confused with the great White Throne Judgement which happens after the thousand year millennium), and Christ rewards his servants, the prophets and saints of all time, encompassing all who are saved.

This last point is a very important one because the Dispensationalists adamantly believe that God, the eternal, omnipotent, omnipresent creator of the Universe, somehow 'needs' seven years to reward His Saints. In other words, they believe that a Pre-tribulation Rapture is necessary so that God has enough *time* to decide who inherits what blessings, because there are so many saved people and so many potential blessings to mete out. I'm sure that not everyone who is a Dispensationalist believes in this restriction of God, but we have heard this idea expounded a few times by them.

Dwight Pentecost supports this assessment of God's power. He wrote: " ... certain events predicted for the church after her translation make such an interpretation (i.e. a Post-Trib view of end time events) impossible. These events are: (1) the judgement seat of Christ ... It is impossible to conceive of this event as taking place without the expiration of some period of time."[95] And while we are sure the Lord would be grateful to Pentecost, and other like-minded thinkers, for the opportunity their eschatology affords Him to take His time in rewarding His Saints (instead of making 'rash decisions' and doing it all at once as the Scripture says), it is simply not necessary. The Lord God is omnipotent, omniscient, and omnipresent! He could reward everyone in the twinkling of an eye if He wanted to, and we believe that He will.

What is truly sad about this is that Dr. Stanton, and the other Dispensational teachers, are willing to use the same kind of non-biblical logic and twisting of Scripture in order to prove Matthew 24 is purely for the Jews during the Tribulation and not Believers as a whole. In the process, what you get is not a sound exegesis of God's Word but a vain attempt by some people trying desperately to make what is biblically untenable and scripturally unsound appear doctrinal, literal and prophetic.

Both 1 Thessalonians and Matthew 24 are mentioned in the direct context of Christ's and Paul's explanation of certain end time events.

---

[95] J. Dwight Pentecost, Things To Come: A Study In Biblical Eschatology, pg. 205.

There is no reason to believe that the resurrection somehow precedes the events in Matthew when, in reality, they are fulfilled when Christ returns. There is also no reason to believe that one passage is 'meant for the Jews' and another is 'meant for the Gentiles;' that one applies to those raptured before the Tribulation and the other represents a security for those (i.e. Jews) left behind after it. Scripture bears this out, despite Dispensational interpretation.

10

Pulling it all Together

As we have written, the Pre-tribulation Rapture doctrine has become a prevalent view of the modern evangelical Protestant church, with its roots firmly planted in the soil of Dispensationalism. Because of this, the question needs to be asked whether those who believe in the Pre-Trib Rapture have learned it through a diligent, unwavering, study of the Bible, or, were they taught it?

Everyone who considers him or herself a Pre-Tribulationist needs to be honest with themselves and ask this question. If they are truthful, we guarantee that they will have to admit that they were taught it and didn't come to it through their own study of Scripture; with the exception of its originator.

Some people will, no doubt, object to this claim, but honest self-examination will bear out the truth of what we say. The authors, also, were once Dispensationalists who believed in the Pre-Trib Rapture, having been taught it in church, and not through our own study of Scripture. And we are certain that every Pre-Trib author we have quoted in this volume was also taught it, from LaHaye to Stanton, to Pentecost, to Chafer, to Scofield, as well as the rest.

When you read the Scriptures without a Dispensational bias, you will more than likely come to a Post-Trib Resurrection point-of-view; unless, like the Amillennial and Post-millennial, you do not believe there will be a specific time of tribulation that is to occur in the future. It was our questioning of this doctrine, and our study of the Bible, which eventually led us to the rejection of these teachings because we discovered that they were not truly founded upon Scripture. We pray that our readers will consider this, and scrutinize what we say through their own diligent study of the Word.

This is your duty, and your obligation, according to Scripture (2 Timothy 2:15).

In this chapter we intend to pull together all of the relevant texts which unearth the entire revelation of the Resurrection, and answer the all-encompassing question, "When will it take place?" We begin by focusing on 1 Thessalonians 4:13-18, which everyone agrees is the main text used by the Dispensationalist in the explanation of the Rapture. "But we do not want you to be uninformed, brothers, about those who are asleep, that you may not grieve as others do who have no hope. For since we believe that Jesus died and rose again, even so, through Jesus, God will bring with him those who have fallen asleep. For this we declare to you by a word from the Lord, that we who are alive, who are left until the coming of the Lord, will not precede those who have fallen asleep. For the Lord himself will descend from heaven with a cry of command, with the voice of an archangel, and with the sound of the trumpet of God. And the dead in Christ will rise first. Then we who are alive, who are left, will be caught up together with them in the clouds to meet the Lord in the air, and so we will always be with the Lord. Therefore encourage one another with these words."

Reading these verses, the first thing we notice is that the key element of time is not mentioned at all. In fact, neither seasons, nor months, days nor even years are spoken of; it doesn't even touch on the key question of whether or not this event takes place before, during, or after the events of the Tribulation. That's because Paul is speaking of it in terms of the *process* of the resurrection, with the Lord descending " ... from heaven with a cry of command, with the voice of an archangel, and with the sound of the trumpet of God" and the dead in Christ rising first (verse 16). Then Paul tells the Thessalonians (verse 17) " ... we who are alive, who are left, will be caught up together with them in the clouds to meet the Lord in the air, and so we will always be with the Lord."[96]

1 Thessalonians 4:17 represents one of the key points of the Rapture debate. People from Darby to Pentecost and LaHaye have used it as one of their chief texts to prove a Pre-Trib event. Yet, as mentioned in the previous chapter, they have confused process with timing and, presuming their eschatological view is right,

---

[96] This event comprises the Resurrection of the just.

they believe this verse somehow validates their presuppositions.

A less impassioned look at 1 Thessalonians 4:13-18, however, reveals that it says nothing of the kind. It is the *process* of the resurrection/rapture that is in view here, not the timing. So, whether a person is Pre, Mid, or Post-Trib, these verses themselves are meaningful, in large part, because of the sense that Paul gave them—for the comfort of believers, and not to settle any eschatological debate.

There are, however, a few verses that do plague and grieve your average Pre-Tribulationist because they completely undermine their eschatology. In fact these verses are so at odds with their views that it makes it hard for them to maintain the voracity of their ideas. It's why, in fact, LaHaye says, "Jesus our Lord will **finish** (our emphasis) His second coming by descending in the midst of the Battle of Armageddon to conquer the world and usher in His wonderful 1,000-year kingdom of peace."[97]

Finish his Second Coming? To LaHaye, apparently, when the Bible speaks of Jesus'

---

[97] Tim LaHaye, The Rapture: Who Will Face the Tribulation?, pg. 12.

return it is not speaking about a single event, but, a multi-phased event like the one Todd Baker put forth in his explanation of the first resurrection.

Again, the Dispensationalist's claim of being biblical 'literalists' needs to be questioned at this point. By understanding the return of Christ in two parts, against Scripture, LaHaye and company demonstrate that their literalism has limits. Willing to take God at His word, that salvation is by grace alone, through faith alone, in Christ alone, they then jump the rails with both feet because of the necessity to protect their cherished Pre-Trib Rapture doctrine. Yet LaHaye has the temerity to warn people about the dangers of doing what he just did, namely failing to take the Word of God literally, telling readers that, "The study of prophetic passages is not difficult when we take the Bible literally whenever possible. If, however, a person begins to spiritualize or allegorize the text, he is hopelessly doomed to confusion and error."[98]

Ironically he does this right after quoting the very verses which undermine his own position and the entire Pre-Trib view, forcing him and others to come up with the flawed view

---

[98] Ibid. pg. 239

that the second coming of Christ is really a two-part event. These verses are found in Revelation 20:1-5, which say, "Then I saw an angel coming down from heaven, holding in his hand the key to the bottomless pit and a great chain. And he seized the dragon, that ancient serpent, who is the devil and Satan, and bound him for a thousand years, and threw him into the pit, and shut it and sealed it over him, so that he might not deceive the nations any longer, until the thousand years were ended. After that he must be released for a little while. Then I saw thrones, and seated on them were those to whom the authority to judge was committed. Also I saw the souls of those who had been beheaded for the testimony of Jesus and for the word of God, and those who had not worshiped the beast or its image and had not received its mark on their foreheads or their hands. They came to life and reigned with Christ for a thousand years. The rest of the dead did not come to life until the thousand years were ended. This is the first resurrection."

Here we have a concise explanation of the immediate events which occur when Christ returns. We see an angel coming down and taking hold of Satan, manhandling him as if he were a common criminal instead of the powerful being he is. This shows the sovereign control of God in all things, even in the terrible events which He purposed to come to pass upon the Earth during the Tribulation. God could certainly dispose of Satan at any time but, for His own purposes, He chooses to allow him to continue in his wickedness until the time He has appointed for his defeat.

In verse 4 we are then told that John sees thrones set up. The implication is that these thrones are upon the Earth, and the judgement, which is given to those on the thrones, is to be exercised here. He then sees the Saints, who were beheaded during the Tribulation, and says that these will rule with Christ during the Millennium.

Then, in verse 5, we are told that, "The rest of the dead did not come to life until the thousand years were ended … " This could only be the wicked dead because, in verses 11-15, it is revealed that the wicked are judged, and then thrown into the lake of fire for eternal torment after the end of Jesus' thousand-year reign.

Finally, at the end of verse 5, the resurrection John has just explained is given the title "the first resurrection." It is not the second resurrection, which is what it would amount to if the dead were raised in Pre-Trib Rapture nor is it the second phase of Christ's return. It "is the return," and it "is the first resurrection."

Other verses which agree with this are John 11:24, which says that the resurrection will be at *the last day*, and John 6:39, which says the same thing. This verse is in fact Jesus' very own teaching. He says, "For I have come down from heaven, not to do my own will but the will of him who sent me. And this is the will of him who sent me, that I should lose nothing of all that he has given me, but raise it up on **the last day**" (John 6:38-39; emphasis ours).

This is what Jesus taught, what His disciples believed (in the case of Martha: see again John 11:23, 24), and what the Apostle John taught in Revelation 20:5.

Jesus also says that the resurrection occurs at the end of the Tribulation in Matthew 24:29-31. "**Immediately after** the tribulation of those days the sun will be darkened, and the moon will not give its light, and the stars will fall from heaven, and the powers of the heavens will be shaken. Then will appear in heaven the sign of the Son of Man, and then all the tribes of the earth will mourn, and they will see the Son of Man coming on the clouds of heaven with power and great glory. And he will **send out his angels with a loud trumpet call**, and they will gather his elect from the four winds, from one end of heaven to the other" (emphasis ours).

Dispensationalists will, no doubt, counter by saying that the 'elect' spoken of here are the Jewish remnant. Unfortunately, the only justification they have for this assertion is the weak one given by Stanton when he, without biblical support, says it is valid because it is " … in keeping with the Jewish content of the passage … ,"[99] something we addressed earlier.

Some would also argue that there was a resurrection before it. They site Matthew 27:52-53, which describes a resurrection that followed Christ's death on the Cross. In these verses, the Bible says "The tombs also were opened. And many bodies of the saints who had fallen asleep were raised, and coming out of the tombs after his resurrection they went into the holy city and appeared to many."

There are many possible explanations for this event, along with many theories. Unfortunately we are unable to fully explain the significance of this event in the present volume. We do, however, maintain that this resurrection was not "the first resurrection" described in

---

[99] Gerald B. Stanton, Kept From the Hour: Biblical Evidence for the Pretribulational Return of Christ, pg. 62.

Revelation, for the reason that "many" Saints were brought back to life, but not all. Also, we know that the first resurrection happens when Christ comes back, not before He ascends to the Father, which is the case in Matthew 27.

Furthermore, Christ, and the angel who spoke to John, would be making a liar out of him by allowing him to call the events at the end of Tribulation "the first resurrection" instead of the second. Most likely, therefore, this passage is a foreshadowing, or taste, of what is to come at the end of the age.

To briefly sum it up, the first resurrection is the one described in Matthew 24:29-31 and supported by Revelation 20:1-5 because it happens at the last day, the last day being the day of Christ's return. Since Christ returns *immediately after* the tribulation it cannot occur before and still be called *the first resurrection*.

This is further confirmed when one reads, 1 Thessalonians 4:13-18, 1 Corinthians 15:51-52, and Matthew 24:29-31 which are speaking about the same event. In 1 Thessalonians and 1 Corinthians Paul is explaining *how* the resurrection is to take place, which he does for good reason.

The Thessalonian Saints, as we mentioned earlier, were troubled by the death of some of their loved ones. Paul took this opportunity to comfort them, telling them that there is going to be a resurrection, and that all the dead in Christ shall be raised up with the living. He wasn't necessarily trying to explain an eschatological truth; all he was describing was the *process* of the resurrection, not the timing of it. He was telling them that it was going to occur and that the believers should not mourn for their loved ones as being lost for good.

In 1 Corinthians Paul is actually battling heresy, a heresy so vile that the men propagating it actually denied the Resurrection altogether! In chapter 15 he takes a fairly lengthy time to dispel this wicked lie and to teach the exact truth of the resurrection. He says that it is part of the Gospel (verses 1-10), tells us the necessity of the proclamation of the resurrection and the implications of denying this truth (verses 11-19), and then comforts us by detailing the assurance we ought to have as believers. He also mentions the application the resurrection ought to have in our lives (verses 20-34) before closing with an exposition as to how the resurrection is to happen, and an exhortation to abound in the work of the Lord because of this truth (verses 35-58).

In verse 52 Paul covers the timing of the resurrection by saying that it happens at "the last trumpet." This is also covered by Jesus Christ in Matthew 24:29-31. It is here we read about how Christ descends from Heaven in the clouds, and then sends His angels to gather the elect at the sound of a trumpet: "Immediately after the tribulation of those days the sun will be darkened, and the moon will not give its light, and the stars will fall from heaven, and the powers of the heavens will be shaken. Then will appear in heaven the sign of the Son of Man, and then all the tribes of the earth will mourn, and they will see the Son of Man coming on the clouds of heaven with power and great glory. And he will send out his angels with a loud trumpet call, and they will gather his elect from the four winds, from one end of heaven to the other."

This lines up with 1 Thessalonians 4:16-17 which explains that Christ comes down from Heaven with a shout and the trump of God and the dead in Christ shall rise first, bringing the living with them to resurrection glory. "For the Lord himself will descend from heaven with a cry of command, with the voice of an archangel, and with the sound of the trumpet of God. And the dead in Christ will rise first. Then we who are alive, who are left, will be caught up together with them in the clouds to meet the Lord in the air, and so we will always be with the Lord" (1 Thessalonians 4:16-17).

1 Corinthians 15:52 gives us even more information, explaining that not every Believer is going to "sleep" or die physically, as was mentioned in 1 Thessalonians 4, but they shall in fact be changed. He says it happens, "in a moment, in the twinkling of an eye, at the last trumpet. For the trumpet will sound, and the dead will be raised imperishable, and we shall be changed" (1 Corinthians 15:52).

Pulling it all together we get a very good picture of this portion of end time prophecy. Immediately after the Tribulation Christ descends from Heaven as was foretold by the angels who met the disciples after Christ had ascended: "And when he (Jesus) had said these things, as they were looking on, he was lifted up, and a cloud took him out of their sight. And while they were gazing into heaven as he went, behold, two men stood by them in white robes, and said, 'Men of Galilee, why do you stand looking into heaven? This Jesus, who was taken up from you into heaven, will come in the same way as you saw him go into heaven'" (Acts 1:9-11).

How did the disciples see him go? Physically, visibly, up through the clouds, and directly from the Earth. If all of this is true, then we can conclude that Christ will come back in reverse order, which is exactly what all of the relevant texts describe. Not once, however, is there even a hint of a 'secret, invisible, and sudden rapture' or return taking place or anticipated before his physical return.

Now, in the midst of Jesus' return, a trumpet is sounded, heralding the angels to gather those who are Christ's, the dead and the living, to His presence where they are glorified with the Lord. Note, once more, that there is no mysterious gap of seven years in any of this.

1 Corinthians 15:20-24 says, "But in fact Christ has been raised from the dead, the first fruits of those who have fallen asleep. For as by a man came death, by a man has come also the resurrection of the dead. For as in Adam all die, so also in Christ shall all be made alive. But each in his own order: Christ the first fruits, then at his coming those who belong to Christ. Then comes the end … "

Where is the seven year interlude in Paul's exposition? It's not there, **because it does not exist.** This notion, like others from the Dispensational camp, was fabricated almost 200 years ago, not by proper biblical exegesis, but by Dispensational theology.

In Revelation 14:14-20 John is shown a picture of the harvesting of the earth at the last day and the two reapings which occur simultaneously on it. "Then I looked, and behold, a white cloud, and seated on the cloud one like a son of man, with a golden crown on his head, and a sharp sickle in his hand. And another angel came out of the temple, calling with a loud voice to him who sat on the cloud, 'Put in your sickle, and reap, for the hour to reap has come, for the harvest of the earth is fully ripe.' So he who sat on the cloud swung his sickle across the earth, and the earth was reaped. Then another angel came out of the temple in heaven, and he too had a sharp sickle. And another angel came out from the altar, the angel who has authority over the fire, and he called with a loud voice to the one who had the sharp sickle, 'Put in your sickle and gather the clusters from the vine of the earth, for its grapes are ripe.' So the angel swung his sickle across the earth and gathered the grape harvest of the earth and threw it into the great winepress of the wrath of God. And the winepress was trodden outside the city, and blood flowed from the winepress, as high as a horse's bridle … "

An individual sitting on the cloud, and appearing to be "the Son of man" with a golden crown upon his head, does the first reaping. We can conclude by the description of this figure that it is none other than the Lord Jesus Christ Himself. Next we are told that the earth was reaped, but it is not revealed to us where those who are reaped at this time are sent. We are, however, given a greater disclosure of the second reaping.

The ones who are partakers of the second harvesting are described as *"grapes"* which are "fully ripe." An angel thrusts in his sickle and collects the grapes but, instead of having some indeterminate location, they are cast "into the great winepress of the wrath of God."

By being "fully ripe" we understand that this means these peoples' sin has reached its zenith. They are thus ready to be removed and punished for their lawlessness, which God demonstrates by treading His winepress, with them underneath His feet (see also Isaiah 63:3-4 where the Lord says "I have trodden the winepress alone, and from the peoples not one was with me; I trod them in my anger and trampled them in my wrath; their lifeblood spattered on my garments, and stained all my apparel. For the day of vengeance was in my heart, and my year of redemption had come.")

We know that this is taking place at Christ's return because this text tells us that " … the harvest of the earth is fully ripe" (Revelation. 14:15). Harvests only happen at the *end* of the growing season, not before. Christ validates this in Matthew 13:39, " … the harvest is the end of the world; and the reapers are the angels."

Although some might contend with us over this, we believe that the event we see in Revelation 14:14-20 is also in Matthew 13:24-30 which says, " … The kingdom of heaven may be compared to a man who sowed good seed in his field, but while his men were sleeping, his enemy came and sowed weeds among the wheat and went away. So when the plants came up and bore grain, then the weeds appeared also. And the servants of the master of the house came and said to him, 'Master, did you not sow good seed in your field? How then does it have weeds?' He said to them, 'An enemy has done this.' So the servants said to him, 'Then do you want us to go and gather them?' But he said, 'No, lest in gathering the weeds you root up the wheat along with them. Let both grow together until the harvest, and at harvest time I will tell the reapers, Gather the weeds first and bind them in bundles to be burned, but gather the wheat into my barn."

Notice that the man specifically commands his servants in the parable in Matthew to let the tares and the wheat grow together *"until the harvest."* It is at that time that the wheat and tares will be separated by God, through the agency of angels.

Explaining this, the Lord says, " ... The one who sows the good seed is the Son of Man. The field is the world, and the good seed is the sons of the kingdom. The weeds are the sons of the evil one, and the enemy who sowed them is the devil. The harvest is the close of the age, and the reapers are angels. Just as the weeds are gathered and burned with fire, so will it be at the close of the age. The Son of Man will send his angels, and they will gather out of his kingdom all causes of sin and all law-breakers, and throw them into the fiery furnace. In that place there will be weeping and gnashing of teeth. Then the righteous will shine like the sun in the kingdom of their Father. He who has ears, let him hear" (Matthew 13:37-43).

This comes from Christ's own teaching on what is to happen at the last day. He never said He takes His crop and leaves to celebrate with it for seven years. He never says He does only a partial reaping and will return later to finish the job (i.e. to recover the 'Jewish remnant' as Dispensationalists claim). Nor does He say it takes Him any length of time to determine the rewards His servants will receive.

There can, therefore, be **no division** between the resurrection and His Second Coming, or even between Gentile believers and Jewish believers. All who are in Christ are **one body**, and are gathered together in glory, while the wicked are gathered together for condemnation.

We know this because Jesus says that the good seed, which are the children of the Kingdom (Believers), are harvested as are the weeds (non-Believers). The weeds are then thrown into the furnace, as described here, while the wheat is gathered into His barn. These are symbolic ways for the Lord to say that the wicked are ordained for everlasting punishment, while the saved are to live with Christ forever in His glory.

He mentions these same truths again in (Matthew 13:47-50), "Again, the kingdom of heaven is like a net that was thrown into the sea and gathered fish of every kind. When it was full, men drew it ashore and sat down and sorted the good into containers but threw away the bad. So it will be at the close of the age. The angels will come out and separate the evil from the righteous and throw them into the fiery furnace. In that place there will be weeping and gnashing of teeth"

When will He sever the wicked from the just? At the **end of the world**, and not before, as those who propagate the Pre-Trib Rapture would have us believe. All of the Scriptures which teach Christ's second coming, when taken together, give us the actual account as to how the First Resurrection will unfold. It is not some mystery which we are kept in the dark about.

The Apostle Paul points out that, " ... you are not in darkness, brothers, for that day (Christ's return) to surprise you like a thief. For you are all children of light, children of the day. We are not of the night or of the darkness" (1 Thessalonians 5:4-5). He then exhorts us, saying, "So then let us not sleep, as others do, but let us keep awake and be sober" (verse 6). Again, if the timing of the resurrection is a secret event, then why are we told to watch? What are we to watch for?

The Bible, as we have shown, is plain and straightforward about the First Resurrection. It is quite tragic that some people, however, have created a theological system (Dispensationalism) that has imposed a "secret" Pre-Trib Rapture over the text of Scripture where none exists.

LaHaye claims that the reason they believe in the Pre-Trib view is because, " … it fits so well all the Bible passages that touch on end-time events … ,"[100] but, as we just proved, those very passages he speaks of actually deny the Pre-Trib Rapture in every way.

In his book, LaHaye wrote a chapter called 'The Pre-Tribulation Rapture: Believe it!' In it, he tries to explain why someone *must* believe the doctrine he espouses. Like U.S. President Woodrow Wilson, LaHaye gives us his own version of The Fourteen Points as to why the Pre-Trib Rapture, in his opinion, is the only viewpoint to be held. These reasons, however, do not do any justice to the teachings of Scripture, or serve to advance his views.

It is not our intent, at this time, to go into great detail about this chapter of LaHaye's book. We will, however, mention some of what he says in order to show how it does not square with Scripture. If you would like to investigate this claim for yourself, we encourage you to pick up

---

[100] Tim LaHaye, The Rapture: Who Will Face the Tribulation? pg. 133.

a copy of his book and see if our criticism is justified.

One of the proofs LaHaye offers to validate his view is, " ... The pre-Tribulation view is the most logical view of second coming scriptures when taken for their plain, literal meaning whenever possible ... Many of the details of the second coming must be pieced together from various passages of Scripture, no matter what view you take. The pre-Trib position finds a logical place for every second-coming passage. Like a completed puzzle, all the pieces fit. As Dr. Walvoord notes, It is rather significant that, without any attempt to establish uniformity in eschatology, the Bible Institute movement of America is predominantly premillennial and pretribulational. This has come from taking Scripture in its plain, ordinary meaning and explaining it in this sense. By contrast, educational institutions that have approached the Bible creedily tend to make Scriptures conform to their previously accepted creed with the result that most of them are liberal or, if conservative, tend to be amillennial."[101]

---

[101] Ibid. pg. 135.

In other words LaHaye's 'proof' is merely his idea that the passages, which speak of the Second Coming, all fit together in their literal meaning to 'prove' a Pre-Trib Rapture. But, instead of actually quoting those passages of Scripture to back them up he defers to Dr. John Walvoord, who is actually quite wrong in what he says.

Walvoord, for his part, presumes that the seminary movement in America was not a unified body in their eschatological outlook. Yet he fails to mention that Dispensationalists started the movement itself, many of whom came out of the Niagara Falls conferences in the late 1800's.

Furthermore, to make the statement that institutions, who have 'creeds' as their foundation are more likely to be liberal or amillennial, is also seemingly disingenuous, considering the fact that *all* seminaries (that we are aware of) have doctrinal statements (or 'creeds') which mention their prophetic positions, even those that are Dispensational!

The Dallas Theological Seminary, for example, of which Dr. Walvoord served as president, beginning in 1952, says in its doctrinal statement, "We believe that the dispensations are stewardships by which God administers His purpose on the earth through man under varying responsibilities. We believe that the changes in the dispensational dealings of God with man depend on changed conditions or situations in which man is successively found with relation to God, and that these changes are the result of the failures of man and the judgements of God."[102]

Referring to the Pre-Trib Rapture, it says, "We believe that the translation of the church will be followed by the fulfillment of Israel's seventieth week ... during which the church, the body of Christ, will be in heaven."[103]

The interesting thing is that Lewis Sperry Chafer, a student of C.I. Scofield, established the Dallas Theological Seminary in 1924 and its doctrinal statement was officially adopted in 1925. This means that it was *already* built upon Dispensational footings long before Walvoord showed up on the scene. As mentioned earlier it was C.I. Scofield, who is largely responsible for the dissemination of Dispensationalism via his famed Scofield Study Bible.

---

[102] Article V—The Dispensations, www.DTS.org.

[103] Ibid.

Continuing to quote Walvoord, LaHaye says, "The pretribulational interpretation allows the interpreter of both the Old and New Testaments to establish an order for the end time events that makes sense. While many details may not be revealed, the major events of the end time as commonly held by pretribulationalists can be established. By contrast, it would be difficult to find two posttribulationalists who agree on any system of events relating to the end time ... The evident trend among scholars who have forsaken pretribulationism for posttribulationism is that in many cases they also abandon premillennialism. For those who wish to think consistently and logically from principles to interpretation, the options continue to be (1) a pretribulational rapture followed by a premillennial return of Christ to the earth, or (2) abandoning both for a posttribulational rapture and a spiritualized millennium."[104]

LaHaye continues in his defence, this time by sighting Walvoord's resume. He says, "Dr. Walvoord, now in his nineties, has been a Bible scholar more than 60 years and personally knows most of the living scholars on this subject.

---

[104] Tim LaHaye, The Rapture: Who will Face the Tribulation?, pg. 135-136.

He warns that 'it is not uncommon for scholars who defect from pretribulationism in favor of posttribulationism to also defect in their doctrine of the inerrancy of Scripture.' I would add that some reject the pre-Trib position because it is not spelled out in detail in one single passage, but they often end up with a position more complex and less logical and not in keeping with the plain sense of Scripture."[105]

Notice, again, the tactic of scaring people into believing the Pre-Trib position by claiming that there is a danger of becoming a heretic if you deviate from their eschatology. We don't believe that this technique is very helpful for the purposes of having an honest debate on the material before us. They blatantly say that if you come to a non-Pre Trib position on this subject, you also stand a good chance of believing that God's Word is also errant and cannot be trusted!

One of the major difficulties with this kind of reasoning, however, is that, as we have already showed, the Dispensational Pre-Trib position is only about 200 years old. If you follow this line of thought closely, then you have to wonder how the Reformers, Puritans, and those who follow in their theological lineage,

---

[105] Ibid., pg 136.

ever survived the pull to become heretical due to a lack of Premillenial Pre-tribulationalism?

LaHaye reasons this same way all throughout this chapter of his book. In fact, he does not mention any passage to support his belief in a Pre-Trib Rapture in this chapter which, as his title claims, must be believed. By the end of it, you are left with the sense that it must be believed, not because the Bible teaches it, but because LaHaye, Walvoord, and others say so.

That, however, is not the path of biblical scholarship. As Christians we are commanded to study the Scriptures (2 Timothy 2:14-16), to desire the pure milk of the word (1 Peter 2:2), in order to grow in grace and knowledge of our Lord Jesus Christ by effective study (2 Peter 3:14-18).

We conclude by saying that the Scriptures clearly testify (abundantly) to a Premillennial return of Christ with a Post-Tribulation Rapture. We have seen that there are only two resurrections which are identified in the Bible, and that the first one is a resurrection of the just and happens upon Christ's return (Revelation 20:1-6), while the second one is a resurrection of the wicked, resulting in damnation (Revelation 20:11-15).[106]

The Lord clearly teaches that the Resurrection will happen at the last day (John 6:38-39), and that this is identified abundantly in His parables and the vision which is recorded for us in John's Revelation (Matthew 13:24-30, 37-43, 47-50 and Revelation 14: 14-20). Matthew 24:29-31 specifically declares that the Resurrection will take place immediately after the Tribulation, and this verse is directly connected to Paul's revelation of the resurrection in 1 Corinthians 15:51-53 and 1 Thessalonians 4:13-18. These verses, together, teach us that the resurrection is immediately *after* the Tribulation (Matthew 24:29), that Christ descends (Matthew 24:29; 1 Thessalonians 4:16), the Last Trump (also known as the Trump of God) will be sounded (Matthew 24:31; 1 Corinthians 15:52; 1 Thessalonians 4:16), the dead shall rise first, then we which are alive shall be caught up (1 Thessalonians 4:16-17; 1 Corinthians 15:52), by the angels (Matthew 24:31), in the twinkling of

---

[106] Christ, in John 5:28-29, speaks exclusively about two resurrection: " ... for an hour is coming when all who are in the tombs will hear his voice and come out, those who have done good to the resurrection of life, and those who have done evil to the resurrection of judgement."

an eye and our bodies will be changed from corruption to incorruption (1 Corinthians 15:52-53).

All of this constitutes the First Resurrection which the Bible plainly and, literally, teaches. Our prayer is that Christians would lay aside their man-made theologies and gain God-made ones that arise from the text of His Holy Word. We, as good stewards of the Master's truth, can do no more. May God, we pray, forbid us to do any less!

www.ingramcontent.com/pod-product-compliance
Lightning Source LLC
Chambersburg PA
CBHW071526040426
42452CB00008B/901